come by here

come by here

My Mother's Life

CLARENCE MAJOR

John Wiley & Sons, Inc.

Published by John Wiley & Sons, Inc., New York
Published simultaneously in Canada

Design and production by Navta Associates, Inc.

ISBN 0-471-41518-9

Printed in the United States of America

10 9 8 7 6 5 4 3 2 1

Someone's singing, Lord, come by here.
Someone's praying, Lord, come by here.
Someone's crying, Lord, come by here.
Someone needs you, Lord, come by here.
Send a blessing, Lord. Come by here.
Come by here, Lord,
Come by here.

—Traditional Negro Spiritual

Preface

A strong bond existed between mother and infant. What more intimate relationship could possibly exist? After all, the infant's entire being was formed inside the mother. Her rhythm, her blood, her heartbeat, her nerves formed his universe. Once born, the infant remained dependent for some time.

In significant ways the infant was like the mother, in other ways not like the mother at all. He came out already a separate individual, a stranger, a different gender and a different color. The infant was born not only stranger to Mother but stranger to self. With pride Mother saw herself in the child's face.

Yet, stranger the child remained. The mother noticed this as the child grew. She said, Who is this familiar stranger? How has this unknown person come into my life? Is this the part of myself that I have been unable to see?

My mother saw me before I saw her. My first sense of self was reflected in her eyes. She and I could not have had a closer, more intimate mother–son relationship, yet we were two very different individuals. We had to adjust to each other, learn each other's ways.

Nevertheless, in terms of temperament and personality, during my early years, my mother remained as much a mystery to me as I must have been to her. This mystery for me was fed by her absence. Soon a greater shroud of mystery closed around my memory of her. That mystery grew and was only dislocated when she visited my sister and me at her parents' home where we were living. The visits were more painful than pleasant.

I remember one visit in particular. She was there for a few days. I was so shy that I had hardly spoken to her. But I was profoundly aware of her presence, and I wanted to talk to her but words would not come. Then one night she left while we were asleep. Perhaps she kissed us as we slept. I don't know. If she did it hardly counted, since we were not aware of it. Years later Mother explained that she had given the manner of departure some thought and concluded that leaving in this way was best. But at the time, it was beyond my understanding.

Children all want as much love as they can get from their parents. They need their parents more than parents need them. I could not imagine my unbearably lovely mother in the context of domestic violence and divorce. With considerable success and without any loss of her innate dignity, she also struggled as a single parent of two, then three children. She knew poverty on intimate terms without ever resorting to public assistance. All of these factors together carried implications larger than her life. They were some of the mosaic parts at the core of the American experience, and spoke profoundly of it. I had yet to see that.

Early on for me there was the self that was actively involved in his own life; then there was the other self, a kind of twin passive self, standing off to the side observing the active self. These were two different types of consciousness. The active one was not as conscious as the passive observer was. My actively conscious self was unquestioningly my mysterious mother's son for, say, the first thirty years. The passive objective self was, too, but being so was only a technicality.

As I grew older, I began to see Mother as a person, a woman with a particular outlook, disposition, traits and longings. From the point of view of my passive observing self, she was no longer necessarily only my mother. Without the growing awareness that came with maturity I would not have been able to look frankly at Mother's life as a young woman.

I had to learn how to see her as Inez, to forget as completely as possible the role I assigned her as my mother. This also meant that my views of her as a person changed. In other words, because of the shift in my own perspective, Mother's habits of character were different from Inez's. She hadn't changed. I had.

The natural distance on her as Mother that I achieved through maturity was surpassed when I willed myself to think in terms of her as Inez. It was a freeing experience. I was less critical and less emotional in my view. Yet I retained memory of Mother, pure and simple. So the exchange and conflict between those two positions of perception fed each other in a creative process.

The fact that I am the son of this particular woman called Inez is, from my point of view, a happy accident. All configurations of parent and child are a roll of the cosmic dice. Inez's life, in its complexity and richness, is ideal raw material. It's a writer's dream. Even so, it took me many years to see what was right in front of my eyes.

It was 1948 and I was eleven. My mother was working as a salesperson in a kiosk at Wabash Avenue—a stop on the Lake Shore Railway line. At that time in Chicago this type of job was not open to black women. My mother was working there as a white woman, but we—my sister and I—didn't know that.

My mother was working the late shift when, one night, we rode with her boyfriend, Darcy, downtown to pick her up. Darcy parked his car a block away and we waited there with the lights turned off.

I said to Darcy, Why are we waiting here? He said, Because your mother is white on her job, and if her boss—or any of her customers—see her getting into the car with us, she might lose her job.

I said, Oh. But still it wasn't clear to me how Mother could be both white and colored at the same time. Although I had known for some time that colored people were looked upon by white people in every negative way possible, I still couldn't imagine why being colored was so bad. Darcy said, We have to be careful. We don't want your mother to get fired, do we? My sister and I both sang *Noooo* at the same time.

That was the first time I learned of my mother's secret life as a white woman. Earlier, when I was five or so and was just beginning to learn about the social line between people called Negroes and people called white, I looked at my mother one day and said to my grandmother, Is Mother white? She said, No, she's light, not white.

So I came to understand there were white people, then there was everybody else. Or to put it another way, it seemed to me that Negroes could be any color from stark white with blue eyes to jet black with a blue cast. Mother somehow could be anything she wanted to be.

Her situation was not an anomaly but a familiar one. She was interchangeably black or white in a region that said in effect she could not be both. In a country where a white woman could give birth to a black child but a black woman could not give birth to a white child, such contradictions make sense only to the participants. So Inez, having no choice, embraced her contradictions.

My idea of Mother expanded. But I had yet to understand what defined a white person—or a black person, for that matter. Little did I know there wasn't even a marker for race in the genetic code, let alone anything of real biological substance behind whiteness or blackness.

My interest in writing about Mother's early life took on greater depth and breadth. But how should I approach the story? I knew the implications of her life were important. Should it be told in the form of a novel or as a biography? After many conversations over the years with Mother about her experiences, I started recording some of our conversations on tape so that I could have a narrative record, in her own voice, to refer to as I began my research.

Rather than writing a novel or a biography of Mother's early life, I chose the memoir form because of its dramatic possibilities and because it allowed a forum for the truth. In it, the larger truth of her experience could be filtered from the facts and preserved in a way not available in either of the other two forms.

The first-person narrative voice was not only inherently proper for the form but it gave me the immediacy I wanted. I also wanted the voice to do two other things. One, to approximate—not mimic—the intimate tone and quality of our conversations. And, two, I wanted to render key events of her early life to the best effect, without giving up entirely her special regional vocabulary.

For a long time, I wondered how to protect the privacy of our relatives. Finally, I decided to change certain names. From archival records of the previous three centuries, I kept the real full names of white and black ancestors on my father Clarence's side only through the generation of my grandparents. On my mother's side I used fictional family names for all of her white ancestors as well as for her black relatives after my grandparents' generation.

In every other way this is Inez's true story.

C. M.

come by here

One

The train's chugging put me to sleep. I was still asleep when the train crossed the Mason–Dixon line at the first peek of daylight. With my eyes closed, I shifted in my seat, turning away from the window toward the man next to me.

Then, fully conscious, I opened my eyes. I felt a sudden fearful chest tightening as I sat up and looked around. The man next to me was white. True, he was the same man who'd sat down beside me just before we pulled out of Chicago last night. But his whiteness now was so stark.

I suddenly realized that I was in an all-white car. The two colored ladies, with peanut butter sandwiches in wax paper, three seats up, and the elderly colored couple, up farther near the door, were now gone.

When you were traveling from the North into the South, at the Mason–Dixon line, the conductor came through the cars and told the Negroes not already sitting in the "colored" car to go there. If you were asleep *he'd gently shake your shoulder and nod to the rear. But the conductor hadn't awakened me.*

I sat there thinking over what had happened. Apparently, to his eyes, I was a white woman traveling alone. The experience was funny and sad. I'd always had a harder time passing for black than I'd had passing for white. My mother was black and her way of life was what I knew as my way. I knew very little about my birth father and his white way of life—if there was such a thing. Whenever I'd let myself start to think about him, an odd and dull pain, like the one in my chest now, stopped me.

But I could think about what was happening to me now. I was having my first experience of being white. And I felt the privilege that came with it. From that moment on I changed. In time, I came to believe that when I was taken to be white I was white. When I was seen as black, I was black.

I was like one of those chameleon lizards I saw on the rocks around our house when I was growing up. Except my color didn't change—people's perception of me changed, depending on the situation. That was how elusive these categories came to be for me.

As that train moved farther south, moving toward Atlanta, each clickety-clickety was taking me back to my miserable life as Clarence's wife. I looked out at the sunny landscape of farmland. And I sat there thinking back on my life, trying to figure out who I was, and who I was becoming.

❦

I was a simple country girl who discovered excitement and promise in the big city, Atlanta, and now in an even bigger city, Chicago. But who I was before leaving Dublinville was still clear in my memory. That girl was put quickly through changes once she was living in the city as a grownup. Everything moved faster here. Before Atlanta and Chicago my dreams were simple. The events in a typical day were also simple and I knew pretty much what each day was likely to bring. City life, though, as exciting as it was, complicated and made everything unpredictable. Discovering the faster pace and more varied day-by-day life of Atlanta challenged me in new ways. They gave me new hope for a fuller, more promising life than I had thought possible.

I closed my eyes. While growing up in Dublinville I knew my sisters wanted to fall in love, marry and have children, to be good wives and good mothers. I remembered vaguely wanting these things but I wanted more. I couldn't remember a time when I didn't believe I could have more. All I had to do was go after what I wanted. That was what Pa always taught me. From an early age I knew I was not like most of the other girls I knew both in my hometown and in boarding school in Athens.

I wanted to improve myself. I'd grown up with the impression that we were better off than most colored families in our town, and we were, but once I moved to Atlanta I saw black families with the kind of material wealth I'd thought only white folks had. It wasn't that I wanted to be wealthy. I wanted to improve who I was as a person, and the city struck me as the place to do it. I wanted to be useful in the world, to live a fuller life.

I also wanted to feel more secure and I came to associate security with the city because that was where the jobs were. If I could earn enough money to buy my own sense of security and independence, then I would not have to ever again be dependent on a man or anybody who might let me down when I most needed help. I knew now, as I sat there on the train with my eyes closed, that I was as deeply disappointed in myself as I was in my husband. I also knew that I had associated him with the possibilities of the big city. Years later I would understand that my attraction to him had everything to do with his flash of self-confidence, his air of independence. These were qualities I rarely saw in other black men. But I couldn't help wondering if his attraction to me had more to do with my skin color than with me myself as the person I was and the person I was becoming.

The train was pulling into Atlanta and I was still deep in thought. I remembered a time when I was five. The old white man Mr. Egmont stopped in front of our house. He sat atop a squeaky wagon pulled by a tired-looking horse. It was his normal stop to sell watermelons and corn. I was outside playing.

After giving me a peach, Mr. Egmont patted the top of my head. As I was eating the peach he said, Child, when you grow up, you go up north where you can be white. You don't have to stay here and be colored all *your life. People here know you colored but, on sight, to a stranger you whiter than I am. And although his words were confusing to me at the time, I never forgot them.*

One of the first things a small child, black or white, learned in the Deep South was that there were these two kinds of people—black and white—and that they were to be kept apart. They were supposed to be two rigidly separated worlds. But it was confusing for me as soon as I became conscious of myself as black, I became conscious of myself also as *white*. No matter how friendly white people were, we were taught that they drew the line when it came to us. I didn't know why. It was just the way life was.

Not that some white people weren't friendly. The white family up the road from us, on the other side, was close to my family. Their name was Knight. They had three children—two boys and a girl, Eddie, Lee and Claudio. They were around the ages of my older brothers and sisters.

I used to go up to the Knights' house all the time, although they didn't have any little children my age. I liked them, and Mr. and Mrs. Knight were crazy about me. Mama and Pa used to get water from their well after ours went bad. From time to time we would give them fruit Mama canned. And they were always giving us things.

At age six, I was getting ready to go to school for the first time. And Pa took me aside and said, Inez, children will tell you that I am not your father. He said, Don't believe them, and don't let them upset you. They don't know any better. A real father, he said, is one who loves you and cares about you. That is a true father. So, I am your true father—just remember that when they start teasing you. I didn't yet know about my birth father, a white man whose family had a long and documented history in Georgia going back to Colonial times.

The colored schoolhouse stood down the hill from the colored Baptist church, called Mt. Zion Baptist. Pa had built both. The little two-room schoolhouse—called the Harriet Beecher Stowe School—that I started going to when I was six had only a few wooden benches for the children to sit on, and a simple table for the teacher.

The children sat on the benches facing the teacher, with a blackboard on the wall behind her. The two rooms joined. One was used for us smaller kids and the other for the older ones. Whenever possible there were two teachers, but it was hard to keep regular teachers there because the pay was so low. Mine was Miss Edna Smith.

I always remembered Pa's words. He'd told me the truth. And he was right. The older kids did tease me about the way I looked, and about that white man, Mr. Webster, being my so-called real father. They said, Why you think you got straight hair? Look at you! Why you think you so *pink*-looking? They wouldn't let me join in their games. And it was a very confusing

6

and painful time. They pulled my hair and hit me—just because I looked different.

My sister, Brenna, tried to fight them off, but she couldn't be with me all the time. They said I had "good hair"—and that was too bad for me. And because my hair was long and straight, it was easy to pull.

But with Pa's little lecture I felt ready for them. I tried to take their talk without letting it get me down completely. Yet it hurt—watching them holding hands and dancing in a circle and singing songs— "Little Liza Jane" and "Little Sally Walker" and such.

They jumped rope and sang count-out songs like "Shoo Turkey"—singing *Did you go downtown? Yes ma'am. Did you get any eggs? Yes ma'am. Did you bring them home? Yes ma'am. Did you cook any bread? Yes ma'am. Did you save me some?*

And they skipped and sang "Just from the Kitchen." *With a handful of biscuits. Shoo fly loo. Oh Miss Mary. Shoo fly loo. Fly away over yonder. Shoo fly loo.* And they played "Go In and Out the Window," too. I wanted so much to play and sing with them.

But I had Pa to go to for comfort—although he couldn't go to school with me to protect me from the kids. I loved Pa. He was good to me and I took comfort in being with him. He was my retreat.

Just after we moved to the new house he was planting a lot of new trees, pecan and fig, pear and plum, and apple trees, then grape vines, on our land. And I followed him around. He liked having me about. When he looked back, I was always there. He'd dig holes, then he'd let me come along behind him, and drop seeds into the holes. That became my job.

One time after the trees started growing, we noticed that one tree was coming up with two different kinds of leaves on it. As it turned out, I had accidentally put apple and pear tree seeds in the same hole. The two trees blended together and bore strange fruit—inedible, but interesting to look at. It was my tree. And rather than getting mad at me for the mistake, Pa, too, liked the peculiar tree, and called it my special tree.

In time, Miss Edna Smith gave up teaching, and became a private nurse. Better pay. She worked full time nursing Mrs. Daphne Webster—the mother of Corrie Webster. Mrs. Daphne had crippling arthritis.

This was the year I was thirteen. On my way to town one day, I was walking by the Webster house at the edge of town when I saw Miss Edna sweeping the front porch.

She waved to me and I waved back. Then she came out into the yard and called me over and said, Inez, you stop here on your way back. I want to see you about something. Then she lowered her voice and said, I have something I want to give you.

When I got back, Miss Edna met me in the yard and handed me an envelope. She said, Now, Inez, these are pictures of *you* when you were an infant. You take these pictures and keep them in a safe place. Don't tell anybody I gave them to you. You hear?

I thanked her, and on the way home, I looked at them. In the pictures, I was a beautiful baby. I hadn't believed that Mr. Webster was my birth father. It was at this point that my resistance to what the kids at school had said was challenged. Still, I was puzzled by these pictures coming out of *his* house. While everybody in town knew about my situation, nobody, black or white, openly talked about it.

What can I say about Corrie Webster? He was involved with Mama before he was married. His mother and father were descendants of plantation owners. After dropping out of the University of Georgia, in Athens, in his first semester, he returned to Dublinville and before long started his secret romance with Mama, a married woman.

When his father, Jestus, died, in 1923, Corrie Webster's mother, Daphne, became head of the family. Corrie and his brother, Edward, inherited the responsibility of running the farm. They mainly grew cotton. Their sister, Miss Minnette, married a local man, and stayed close to her family. The brothers had about fifty Negroes living and working shares on the farm— which was behind the family mansion.

Some years later, Corrie Webster married Nancy Ferguson, also from an old Marietta plantation family. Nancy's grandfather had been a state senator and a gentleman farmer. Corrie Webster had three sons—

Melvin, Owens and Russell—by Nancy Ferguson. Corrie and his family lived in the Webster family mansion with his mother, Old Lady Daphne. Edward and his family lived in the second family home, across the street from the mansion. Both houses had separate quarters for live-in servants, such as cooks and house-keepers, and sharecropping cabins out back for the cotton pickers.

I was sure Corrie Webster's sons knew I was related to them by blood. They always acknowledged my presence and treated me kindly. In fact, I think they were fascinated by me. Whenever we met, they looked at me with great curiosity—carefully going over every inch of my face, hair, neck, and arms.

They were so interested in me that—until I got accustomed to it—their staring made me nervous. Miss Minnette was also extremely interested in chat-ting with me whenever we happened to meet, which was usually in town, when I was picking up the mail at the post office, or buying candy.

Anyway, I hid the baby pictures under the newspaper in the bottom of my drawer. Several weeks later, I asked Mama about them. She didn't give me a straight answer. She said, Aunt Millie, the midwife, had trou-ble trying to deliver you. They had to go get Dr. Tracy. He came in a hurry, she said, and delivered you.

But nobody remembered the exact time of my birth. April 24, 1918, sure, but nobody knew the hour. And nobody could check because all the birth records were burned in a courthouse fire in 1933. The only thing my brothers and sisters remembered was that I wasn't there when they went to bed, but I was when they woke up.

Then, when you were a month old, Mama said, the doctor came back to check on how you were doing. His wife, Miss Josephine, came with him. And it was at that time that Miss Josephine took the photographs of you, Mama finally said. I remember her with that camera. I suspected all along that Old Lady Daphne put her up to it. Why she wanted photographs, I don't know, Mama said. But that's how they ended up in that house.

Mama had never seen them before now. They had been in Old Lady Daphne's possession for thirteen years when Miss Smith took it upon herself to give them to me, probably thinking that they would never be missed, since—chances were—nobody had looked at them in all that time.

Twenty-five years later Mama was visiting me in Chicago. For the first time in my adult life, I was alone with her long enough to get up enough nerve to ask her questions that had been on my mind for years. The main thing I wanted to know about was her affair with my birth father. I said, How can you be sure, Mama, that Corrie Webster was my father? Pa had enough white in him to have been my father. She said she knew because she and Pa had not had anything to do with each other for more than a year. They had stopped sleeping together.

Then I wanted to know if I was conceived without love. She said, I believed your father loved me. He acted like it and he told me so, many times. And I was crazy about him, she said, and he was good to me. But people would not put up with our being together, she said. We couldn't marry, even if I had gotten a divorce. We knew that. So we met in secret for a little over two years.

The affair, she said, didn't continue after you were born. A few years later, he got married and had three sons. You are Corrie Webster's oldest child, Mama said. His other children, Melvin, Russell and Owens, were all born after you. A lot of people later on didn't know that. They thought Corrie Webster had been stepping out on his wife. But the affair took place long before his wife came into the picture. Oh, she knew about it, and didn't approve, but it was before her time.

Mama didn't seem a bit embarrassed. And there was nothing in the way she was talking that suggested she regretted any of it. In fact she said she was proud that I was her daughter. I am proud, too, she said, that Corrie Webster was your father. You have nothing to be ashamed of, Mama said. And I just looked at her, realizing that the way she felt—about her relationship with Corrie Webster and about my birth—belonged to a time past.

Mama paused, then said, His drinking didn't start till later on, after his sons were born. He was not happy in his marriage. He drank every day till he died.

But he wasn't the only one, she said. There were men

like him, white and black, who just had to drink hard liquor every day. No matter what else they did or didn't do, they got that liquor into their stomachs every day. They would sit in front of the filling station, she said, and pass the bottle around. He was right there with them, and sometimes I saw him when I passed. There was a special look in his eyes. I could tell, just by the way he still looked at me.

I was sorry I'd asked Mama those questions. I now knew things I felt I'd have been better off not knowing. The knowledge was a burden. I wanted Pa to be my father so bad I could taste it. I felt angry that he was not my father, angry because I loved him so much. But I knew that in the best sense Pa was my father and that he loved me.

I was ten, and back home from Atlanta, when I first came face-to-face with my birth father, Mr. Corrie Webster. The first time I talked with him I was in town to pick up the mail. He was dressed in a suit and tie, and sitting on a Coca-Cola crate, in front of the new filling station, talking with some other white men.

He called me over and said, How you doing, Inez? and I said, I'm doing all right, sir. He said, You are a pretty little girl. And I thanked him. He then told me to hold out my hand. And he handed me two nickels and told me to go buy myself some ice cream. I headed straight for Mr. Sherman's drugstore. Mr. Sherman was the pharmacist. He ran his drug business on one side, and on the other, he had Miss Hatty selling ice cream across the counter.

After that first time whenever I spoke with Mr. Webster, he'd say something nice to me like, That's a mighty pretty dress you're wearing. And he'd end by giving me money for candy or something. This became a regular thing. If my sisters were with me he'd give them something, too. I thought he was a very nice man, but I didn't at that time know that he had had anything to do with my birth.

Except for right downtown, none of the streets in Dublinville were paved. The house I was born in in 1918 was on a side street that ran back of the town courthouse. People used to confuse our Dublinville with the Dublin in Laurens County. That was a lumber town with over six thousand population. Our Dublinville was in Oglethorpe County, just a little north of Atlanta, and the population never climbed above five hundred till the 1970s.

The town sat at the bottom of a hill and the main road led down into it and became the main street through town. The old Presbyterian church for white folks—a white frame building built by Pa—was on the eastern edge of town, and across from it was the old manse. Dublinville was a slow-moving, quiet town.

We were the Hulls, a close-knit family. I had three older sisters and two older brothers. The one next to me was Brenna—Brenna Katrina. She was three years older than I was. The next one was six years older. She was Saffrey. Then Albert, called Bert, was two years older than Saffrey. And Wilbur was two years older than Bert. And the oldest girl, Lowella, was one year older than Wilbur.

Two

One afternoon, when I was three and a half, I was in our backyard playing and singing with Brenna and some neighbor children. We sang—*I had a little dog, his name was Trot, he wag his tail into a knot.* And we clapped hands and sang some more. *Willie and Dillie run a race, Dillie fell down and skin his face.* And we kept clapping. *I had a little pig, I fed him slop, he so fat he almost drop. A B C double down D, A B C double down D. Patty cake patty cake baker-man, put the baby in a dishpan—*

Then I suddenly felt sick and sat down on the steps. I didn't know it then but I almost went into a coma. The other kids gathered around me but nobody knew what was wrong.

The next thing I knew, I was in bed between two crisp white sheets and my family was gathered around me. The big pink face of Dr. Harvey Rhys was leaning over me, looking me right in the eyes. Because of the serious way everybody was acting, I felt scared.

Dr. Rhys was a friendly white man with a kindly face. He'd come in the mornings and spend what seemed like a lot of time with me. I was having trouble breathing. My throat was sore and swollen. And I couldn't swallow anything but liquids. Every morning, Dr. Rhys came and gave me a shot and took my temperature. This went on for quite a while. And his son, Egan, who was in medical school, came to check on me every afternoon.

Then one morning I heard a lot of hammering out front. I wondered what was going on but nobody was there to ask. Later, I learned that a white man had come out to the house and nailed up a big sign on our front door that said KEEP OUT OF THIS HOUSE BY ORDER OF THE BOARD OF HEALTH.

Nobody in our family could leave and nobody, except Dr. Rhys and his son, could come in. I heard Dr. Rhys telling Pa that what I had was diphtheria. He said lots of children all over the country were dying from the disease. Because it was dangerous, Mama and Pa had to keep a close eye on me because the inflammation could attack my heart.

He said some people carried the disease in their tonsils but didn't come down with it. Maybe a carrier had coughed in my face and passed it on to me. I understood none of this at the time—only that I was not feeling well.

❧

There was an old woman, Miss Jolie, who brought milk to our house during that time. Rather than bringing it in, like she used to do before my illness, Miss Jolie had to leave the milk on the front porch. She and her husband, Mr. Merl, lived a half-mile down the road south of us and they had Jersey milk cows.

When we needed other things like salt or sugar, Mama would stand in the door and tell somebody what we needed from the general store in town. We had friendly neighbors who didn't mind helping us out since we were all confined to the house. We were the only family we knew of that was confined like that.

When I was four and a half, Pa bought some land, and started building us a new six-room house, about a mile down the highway south of town. He'd work on it between his other house-building jobs. By the time I turned five, we were already living there.

We moved in before he finished it. There was no front porch, no steps, no glass in the windows. Pa had placed screen wire on and made wooden shutters to cover the windows. The glass came pretty soon and Pa put it in. He had also built three fireplaces in the house, one in the front bedroom, one in the living room, and the third one in the back bedroom, the room that later became his room.

I had measles the day we moved in. Because it was raining, Pa brought me to the new house wrapped in a blanket. He handed me in through the window to

Mama. And she put me in bed. And our neighbor Old Man Donoghue cut Pa some long rocks. Then Pa brought them and laid them down at the front door so everybody could step up into and down from the house. These were just make-do steps till Pa had a chance to build a front porch and proper steps.

Mama, in the meantime, made some kind of concoction to rub on my skin, because the itching kept me irritable and miserable. While I was sick with measles, Mama taught me a poem she'd learned as a girl in school. But I believed she just wanted to keep my mind off the itch.

The other thing in her mind was the fact that her own mother, Grandma Lucy, was planning to soon visit us. And Mama wanted me to be able to recite the poem for her mother, just like she herself had recited it years before for her. The poem was about a granny taking a small child on her lap and telling her a story. But I didn't care that much about the poem, and I wasn't particular about learning it to recite for Grandma. But I did learn it, and I guess I never forgot it.

All the while I was ill, Mama worked at making a patch quilt, made from scraps of old coats, overalls, dresses, jackets and shirts. She would sit with me while she worked. I loved the colors. As a matter of fact, Mama made all of our quilts and many chenille bedspreads herself during the years I was growing up.

To get the chenille effect, she would sew heavy

thread through white cloth. She drew her own designs—stars, half-moons, triangles, flowers and circles all over the spread. She made the patterns tell stories, stories about various family members and neighbors. And it was in this way that I passed through my illness.

My own interest in making things, especially things useful and associated with everyday life, clothing for instance, was sparked by Mama's example. Years later I became a professional dressmaker, creating many of my own designs and patterns. The sense of order and fulfillment I got from such work helped to keep me sane at crazy times in my life.

When I was close to five, Aunt Ella's son Ernest—my first cousin—came for me in his buggy and took me to visit for a few days. Aunt Ella Young and Aunt Sara King—two of Mama's sisters—were living in Gresham Town not far from us in Dublinville.

I liked Aunt Sara but I liked Aunt Ella better. I knew Aunt Ella thought I was cute. She'd made a fuss over me and my light skin and my straight hair since I was a baby. I enjoyed the attention. Although I later felt ashamed of this sort of false satisfaction, I could never entirely ignore the fact that I looked different. People wouldn't let me forget. I wanted to blend in and to be accepted despite my color, not because of it.

Aunt Ella had four other children—all dark-complected. The family was living in a big farmhouse, and growing lots of things on their land, while Aunt

Sara was living in a little house down the road a short distance from Aunt Ella. Aunt Sara also had five children. Her daughter, Susie, was my own age.

I was staying with them. And every morning, Susie and I would get up and run up to Aunt Ella's, to see her and her five children. It was at her house that I first saw brown flour. This was a big deal for me. She used it to make delicious biscuits.

One morning as Susie and I were busting out the door, Aunt Sara shouted to us to tell Aunt Ella to send her a *mess* of greens. I'd never heard the word mess used that way before, but Susie and I delivered the message and brought a bundle of greens back to Aunt Sara. The next day, Aunt Sara said, Go tell Aunt Ella to send me a mess of string beans. Every morning it was bring me a mess of this or bring me a mess of that.

Then came the day for Ernest to drive me back home in his buggy. When I was packed and ready, Aunt Sara told me to run up to Aunt Ella's house and kiss her good-bye. Susie ran up there with me. I kissed Aunt Ella and I said, Aunt Ella, I had a good time.

She said she was so glad, and asked me if there was anything I wanted to take home. And I said, Yes ma'am, I'd like to take my mama a *mess* of your brown flour. And she burst out laughing. How could I have known that flour didn't come by the mess? For years, Aunt Ella told that story, to much merriment, when family members gathered.

Because the kids at Stowe gave me such a hard time about my color and hair, when I turned eight, Mama and Pa transferred me to David T. Howard Elementary School in Atlanta. So I moved to Atlanta and stayed with my brother Wilbur and his wife, Carrie. She was good to me. They both were.

This was my first taste of the big city. Even at age eight, I felt and responded to the faster pace. Unlike in my hometown, railroad tracks ran right into the city. More than one bus station, left over from the old stagecoach lines, gave people travel options. Colored and white taxis waited in front of both the railroad station and the bus stations. You could also take a streetcar to just about anywhere within the city limits, although you had to ride in the back. Still, you got where you wanted to go all the same. I knew of two hotels for Negroes and maybe twenty for white people. There was one movie house for Negroes and about five for white people. Talkies would soon be hitting the theaters. Unlike in my hometown, because we were too far out, you could turn on a radio and actually hear people talking. There was already a Negro business district starting up. Later the man I would marry would be a respected member of that community. Negroes even had a place where they could play tennis and another place where they played baseball. Negro baseball was a big attraction. It was all of this and more that made Atlanta so appealing to me.

To make sure the other kids didn't pick on me like

they had in Dublinville, Carrie got this older boy, Blake, to walk me to and from school. He was a student at Howard, too. Blake had lost an eye some kind of way when he was younger. I never called him One-Eyed Blake, but his male friends did. If anybody else called him One-Eyed, he knocked their teeth out.

Blake was tough and rough looking, and he lived in Buttermilk Bottom, which was down the hill below Carrie and Wilbur's, on Pine Place. Nobody ever messed with Blake. He became my regular body-guard. Carrie gave him a nickel a day for the job.

Blake went with me the first day to register. The lady in the office told me that I had to also get a small-pox shot since I'd never had one. That meant an extra trip for Blake and another nickel from Carrie. He escorted me to the nurse's office the next day, and his presence made the shot less painful.

It was exciting to be walking on sidewalks rather than dirt roads. The intersections had STOP signs. I'd never seen so many cars before. Carrie bought food in cans and stored them on shelves in her kitchen. I thought this a much more efficient way to deal with food than the way Mama, and other country people, had to deal with it. I was of that generation that quickly became impatient with country ways.

There were also two other little girls Blake escorted to and from school. So he made fifteen cents a day and that was a lot. He'd meet me at the back door of the house and walk me to school. Then when school was over he'd wait for me outside the entrance.

In fact, one day, when a boy on a bicycle, on Forest Avenue, knocked me down in front of the dime store, and broke my shoulder, and Carrie and Wilbur had to take me to Grady Hospital, Blake came along, too. The doctor put the arm on that side in a sling. Blake took his job seriously. My broken shoulder, oddly enough, was not all that painful. The long time that it took to heal and the awkwardness of managing it were the painful parts. What with my bout with diphtheria, and now a broken shoulder at eight, doctors were becoming a routine part of my life.

But here at David T. Howard, unlike in Dublinville, there were plenty of light-skinned kids, and many of them looked as white as I did. So nobody here picked on me for my color. It wasn't even discussed. Still, Blake was there to protect me from whatever might happen. Girls, and even boys, often wanted to fight. Reasons varied—just being a new face, or you were not in their clique, or you got an *A* and they got a *B* on a writing assignment, or your dress was prettier than theirs.

Meanwhile, Carrie took a lot of pride in dressing me for school. She enjoyed making me look pretty. It was through her that I first came to appreciate my appearance. My ability to accept how I looked was damaged from the beginning of school at Stowe. Now Carrie was showing me that it just might be possible that I was pretty. If so, maybe I should carry myself in a proud manner and learn how to appreciate who and what I was.

I credit Carrie with helping me turn that corner. She used to curl my hair into baby-doll curls. She wanted me to be the prettiest girl in the neighborhood and at school. But with a broken shoulder I felt pretty sad with one sleeve dangling. By the way, the boy who knocked me down did it out of love, or maybe I should say puppy love, because he was also about eight. Running into me like that was just his strange way of expressing his interest in me.

During this time I didn't see much of my quiet, tall, stern brother Wilbur. He was working long hours on a Coca-Cola Bottling Company delivery truck. After work he would go to a car repair shop where he was learning auto mechanics. It was usually night before he got home. Like Pa, he'd taught himself a valuable skill, and he was doing all right in a world that didn't give black men much of a chance at survival. And in later years, Wilbur learned radio mechanics, too, and opened a radio repair shop, which he kept till his death many years later.

The day I left David T. Howard, I was ten years old. This was in my second year. I had to leave because I came down with some kind of paralysis. One of my knees became swollen and twisted. It wouldn't straighten out. It hurt and I had a hard time walking on that leg. The symptoms were like an arthritic condition. Here again, more illness.

As a result, Mama and Pa called in doctors, but nothing they did had any effect on my bent leg. Then

Mama herself made a poultice of vinegar and red mud. She caked my leg with the mixture and let it dry like a cast. This was a formula she'd learned from her mother, who had learned it from her mother. Who knows how far back it went? Maybe it originated in Africa or maybe it had origins among some of her early Native American ancestors. Anyway, in a couple of days or so the swelling went down. My leg was once again as straight as it had ever been. And after the poultice was off, she then rubbed my leg with snake oil.

Unlike in Atlanta, back at home, I had to attend church every Sunday. Maybe God would keep my leg from swelling again. But I found church annoying— with all of that shouting and screaming and hollering. The preacher made it seem like if you didn't come up and shake his hand after his sermon, you were going to die and go to hell. Then, too, in church, my shoes always hurt and the benches were hard. I was also feeling restless being back in the slow pace of our small town.

But going to church was an automatic thing in my family. It was expected of all of us. Naturally, I was baptized, and it took place in Madison. The preacher was dressed in black and his skin was the color of midnight. All the sisters and girls were in white so bright it hurt your eyes. The deacons were in ocean blues or black-blues, and the boys were in earth browns and grays. They stood on shore piously watching and waiting.

27

The preacher and I were standing down in the shallow water of a creek near the church. While he talked to God and I waited, not knowing exactly what to expect, I looked up at the blue sky, half expecting to see some sign of Heaven, an opening, and angels with trumpets. But I had a feeling that what was about to happen to me wasn't going to be fun.

When my attention wandered to the sky, the preacher quickly grabbed my head with both hands, startling me, then dunked me under head first, then brought me up just as quickly. I was blinded, and came up choking and gasping.

I spat water, gagged, and shook like a wet dog. I wanted to, but I didn't cry. I heard a chuckle or two, girls giggling. My eyes were burning. I couldn't see a thing—except the silver light of the bright day. And later, one of the deacons pinned a baptism badge on me. The date on it, *July 10, 1929.*

The discomfort of this experience, and other rituals in and around the church, caused me to feel guilty about not wanting to attend church. I couldn't then imagine not going, but in later years the memory of that discomfort made it easier for me to choose another type of church. Not that there was anything wrong with Mama's church. I was the problem.

I was sixteen now, and attending Union Baptist Institute for colored girls in Athens. Athens was a bigger town than Dublinville, and it sat on a hill hugging the

Oconee River. The downtown area ended at the university.

The white girls were in the Eppy Cobb Institute. In town there were three movie houses for white folks and one for colored. Bus fare around town was a nickel. I went back and forth by way of the Union Bus Station on West Broad Street.

My family had to pay for me to go to that private school. Families often paid tuition with food items, such as smoked hams, or baskets of eggs, or crates of apples, or buckets of figs, or sacks of corn or potatoes, or they paid with a truckload of wood—whatever they had of value.

Pa always tried to make sure he paid for me with real money, but one time he gave the money to the parents of my best friend, Laura Morton. They agreed to pay for both Laura and me with enough food to last the school a whole year.

Unlike my folks, Laura's folks were regular farmers. We owned chickens and hogs—and for a while, before I was born, a cow— but Pa never kept a horse or a mule for plowing. He borrowed one when he needed to plow the garden. After all, he was a carpenter, not a farmer, and a dignified man in all that he did.

During my first school year in Athens, Laura and I stayed in a boardinghouse run by Mrs. Marie James. Mrs. James had only one room to let, and every year she'd rent it out to two girls. It was a pleasant little gingerbread house and I was comfortable there with

Mrs. James and Laura. Mrs. James was like a mother to us and Laura and I were like sisters.

Laura and I went to church service together on Sunday, except for once when her heel was broken. We also walked to and from school together and did our shopping together. I liked her because she had a ready smile and she and I had a lot of the same thoughts about the future. We also liked a lot of the same things in food and clothing and music. Sometimes on the sly—when Mrs. James wasn't around—we practiced dance steps of the Charleston, the Black Bottom and the Camel Walk. Laura and I had fun together. Unlike my own sisters, she and I were close in age.

Having already lived away from home for two years made it easier for me to get used to being on my own there in Athens. It wasn't hard at all. I was already a responsible little lady. I washed my own clothes, cooked my own food. My sister-in-law Carrie had taught me a lot about taking care of myself, and I knew from Mama how to cook and sew.

One time when I was back home for the summer, Mama wanted the mail from town, but Pa—who usually picked it up on his way home—was at work somewhere building a house. The post office didn't deliver mail to people in or even near town, only to folks way out on remote farms.

This was before the time when mail was delivered to a box in front of your house. But Mama didn't know how to drive the car. By then we had a big old dark green Hudson. Saffrey was up the road baby-sitting Miss Claudio's oldest child. And Saffrey couldn't drive, either.

So I told Mama that I'd drive to town and get the mail for her. I wasn't scared to do it. I figured I could drive a car. I knew how to start and stop a car. I'd watched Pa and my brothers. Just at that point, Saffrey came in and told Mama that I could do it. Then I put a pillow in the seat to make myself tall enough to see over the dashboard. What nerve I had at that time!

The main road that ran by our house was not yet paved except as you got close to town. I drove up the gravel road and over the hill, and down into town, then all the way around the courthouse. I stopped the car in front of the post office.

I got out, and on the sidewalk, I stopped to let Mr. Tinsley and his wife, Miss Christy Tinsley, pass. I spoke to them but only she returned my greeting. Mr. Tinsley said, Nez, did you drive that car all the way to town by yourself? I said, Yes sir. And he said, Well, I'll be durned. Mrs. Tinsley smiled and said, You're a brave little girl. I'd always liked her and I could tell she liked me. Then I went in and got our mail from the clerk.

Forty-three years later, I was in Dublinville visiting Mama. One day Miss Christy stopped by to sit for a while with me in the swing. It was early afternoon and Mama was taking her nap. Before Miss Christy got there, I had been just looking at how many new houses

31

had sprouted up alongside the highway since the last time I was here. Each time I came there were more new houses and more people everywhere.

Miss Christy said, Inez, I want to tell you some things. My ears perked up. Something in her tone troubled me and my heart felt like it was swelling. What kind of things?

Miss Christy was pointing. And she said, See that new house down the road? When that white woman Mrs. Handwerk bought that property she also bought the road by her house that led from the highway to the colored cemetery. Miss Christy said, Then Mrs. Handwerk had the whole road plowed up and planted as a garden so the colored folks couldn't use the road to get to the new colored cemetery. I know you got kinfolks buried there. Ada told me.

Miss Christy paused for a moment, then said, About five years ago a white man named Hymie Tomsett moved to Dublinville and bought that land back there around the old colored cemetery. She was now pointing in that direction and I knew well the area she was talking about. The old cemetery was behind the new one.

Miss Christy said, Hymie hired somebody to plow back in there and the tractor driver knocked over your grandmama's gravestone, and a whole lot of others, too. Then your brother Bert came out with a shotgun and he drove the tractor driver away and told him, Don't you never come back here. Miss Christy laughed. And I thought, I like this white woman.

32

Then she told me a story about Mama. Nobody else is going to tell you these things, she said. Your mama left the house before day one morning and was walking toward town. My husband found her where she had stumbled and fell on the side of the road and she couldn't get up, so my husband helped her up and back to the house, then he called Bert.

After Miss Christy left, and after Mama and I finished dinner, I said to Mama, Do you remember leaving the house and falling alongside the road? She said, Yes, I do. Mama, where were you going? I waited for her answer. I really wanted to know. And Mama finally said, I was going home. Then I said, Home? You left home and were walking up the road to town. Then Mama said, When I woke up that morning, this house didn't look like my house.

Later, when I saw Bert, I told him what Miss Christy said about him and the shotgun. And he said, Yeah, they took the road to the new cemetery. We let that slide. But when they started treating the old cemetery like it was nothing, I had to put a stop to it. If Pa was living, them white folks wouldn't have dared touch the ground where his ma is buried.

That's holy ground, he said. You got that right, I said. And I remembered good things Pa told me about his mother, Melanie, a slave girl owned by Judge Hicks of Wilkes County. His was a well-known and respected family in that county. Their ancestors came over from England. Like so many of them they tried to be aristocrats in Virginia before moving on. Some settled in the

Carolinas, others in Georgia. They used up people,
though, to achieve their goal. Unlike many of the slaves,
Melanie had endured. She was our rock and would
always be.

Driving back, I drove just fine until I got to the
house. We had a circular driveway that ran all the
way around our house. I drove past the first driveway, and just as I tried to turn into the second one, I
pressed too hard on the gas, and ran into the garden
fence and tore it down. I hit two or three young
apple trees. The car didn't stop till I was out in the
middle of the garden.

Saffrey came running out to see what happened. I
wasn't hurt and I jumped out. We were scared Pa was
going to have a fit. So before Pa and Bert got home,
Saffrey got some wire cutters and cut the twisted wire
from around the wheels. I got in and backed the car
out of the garden and parked it in the backyard where
it belonged. Saffrey helped me stand the new apple
trees back up straight. We raked up some dirt and
packed it around the base of the trees to try to make
them look normal again.

I was scared although Pa never whipped me. I was
mostly scared of disappointing him and losing his
love. I didn't want him to think poorly of me. I was
worried all the rest of the afternoon, hoping Pa would
never find out.

But, of course, Pa found out anyway. He could see
the damage—to the trees and the car, to say nothing

of the fence. Yet he didn't scold. Instead, he took it to be an accident. After all, I hadn't meant to do it. Right away Pa just went and bought some new fencing and patched the broken places. The trees were okay. And that was the end of it and I was greatly relieved.

Three

Pa was like that. He was a good man. And he was curious about everything. Our house was full of his books—law books that his father, Judge Hicks, gave him. He read the newspaper every day because he was interested in what was going on in the world and in people. Had he had the opportunity for more education, he might have become a scholar or a scientist.

Strangers found him interesting. Beggars and migrating farm workers on the way to Florida to pick fruit, just going farther south for the winter, used to stop by our house for handouts. Many of them got into conversation with Pa and ended up staying for a day or two. These were white men on the move. Many of them were from up north, and they were friendlier than the white men Pa knew in Georgia.

Maybe because they wanted something—I didn't know. They wore their whiteness, all right, but unlike the Georgia white men they didn't wear it like it was a name given them by God. And Pa would always find something to hand each and every one of these men, even if it was only some bread to take along.

Looking back, I think Pa appreciated meeting white men who approached him on equal terms for a change. He never felt inferior to anybody. And he taught us all that we were as good as the next person—not better, but just as good. So it was hard for us to go around looking up to local white folks the way they wanted us to do so that they could believe they were better.

But this was the South long before the civil rights movement of the 1960s, and we knew there were limits to how consistently we could stand up to white folks who were determined to keep us in what they believed to be our rightful place—beneath them—without being cut down. It often seemed that nothing on earth was more important to white folks than this effort.

Mama wondered how these traveling white men knew to stop at our house. Pa said they left a signal like a mark on a tree or a post or left a little piece of string or ribbon tied on a bush so that the next one coming along would know which house was friendly. People called these men tramps. They rode railroad cars when they could, but walked most of the time. And it looked like they always stopped at our house for food. And we always gave them what we could.

These men fascinated Pa. You couldn't pull Pa away from an interesting conversation. He'd sit on the front porch late into the night talking with them about all kinds of things that interested men—Coolidge and Hoover, Hirohito, the World War, the *Titanic*, Babe Ruth, Jack Johnson and such. One thing, though, that they didn't talk about was the sad condition of black people in the South. They always had their bedrolls on their backs and as I said before, sometimes Pa let some of them stay and sleep on the porch.

When it was raining and Pa felt like he trusted a particular man, he'd let the man sleep inside on the hall floor in the front hallway. I remember that one had come all the way down from Canada. And we all were excited by cans of tiny sardines he had with him. He opened one and held it for us to see. None of us had ever before seen sardines that small. He left us three cans.

Many of the men gave us little tokens of gratitude like that. They sometimes gave us children candy. One, who hit the road before daybreak, left three single dollar bills sticking up like bookmarks in a book in the bookcase in the hallway.

Another one came from Philadelphia. He talked a lot about that city and how people there were living. He told us about modern refrigerators and gas stoves, lots of new cars on the streets, people with loud-ringing telephones in their homes.

Pa asked all of these men endless questions about things going on where they came from. He couldn't get enough of their stories. And I often played nearby, on the steps or out in the yard, so I could overhear what Pa and the men were saying. I followed the stories they told with keen interest. Anything that excited Pa that much had to be interesting. And I wanted to be a part of anything that he liked.

Being a deacon in the church, Pa also had the reverend to our house often on Sunday afternoons for dinner. Pa and the preacher would also sit on the front porch and drink some of Mama's homemade wine before dinner while talking men's talk. They talked about the meaning of life, the cotton industry, what the country was coming to, about white folks and racism, about friends and neighbors, the president, what Congress was doing and many other things.

That's the kind of man Pa was. He loved stories and talking. He talked to us kids a lot, too. Unlike other men in Dublinville, Pa took a lot of time with all of his children, but especially with me. Years later, it occurred to me that because his own situation—white father, black mother—was like mine, Pa may have identified with me from the beginning of my life. Maybe in a way he saw himself in me. But I liked believing he mostly liked me for myself.

And he had a sense of humor, too. Once he was trying to teach me the Lord's Prayer so I could recite it before going to bed. Night after night I would repeat the words after Pa. Then one night Pa asked me to say the prayer by myself, but I couldn't do it because I hadn't memorized it.

I'd just been repeating it after him. So one night he wrote out the Lord's Prayer in full on the blank side of the top of a shoebox and attached it with a string to the head of my bed. And he said, "Now, Nez, before you go to bed just get down on your knees and *point* to that sign and say, 'God, there it is!'"

He was like that. One Sunday we were all sitting out on the lawn beside the church waiting for service to start and my Sears Roebuck black patent-leather shoes were hurting my feet so bad I was nearly in tears. When I told Pa, he had a ready answer: Just take them off and put them in your pocket. The fact that going inside the church barefoot was taboo just didn't concern him. I did as he said, although I knew it was wrong. I could tell by Mama's expression that she disapproved, but she didn't say anything. She never did cross Pa in that way. And all during service nobody else even noticed my blasphemy. On the way home I wasn't struck dead by a bolt of lightning from the sky.

Pa thought of himself as a teacher—or maybe I should say as a kind of philosopher. This is an example. I was not yet five. We'd just gotten a radio and I was excited listening to the voices coming out of this box.

Pa said, You think this radio is something. You'll live to see people on a screen talking in Paris or London or New York while you're right here. And you may even live to see the new century come in. And all of his predictions came true. I did live to see the new century come in. Over time the memory of his life and teachings became more and more precious to me.

Pa didn't take any crap, either, and he wouldn't let anybody mess with us. One day three or four prank-playing white boys—the Duncan boys—in a Model-T Ford tried to scare my three sisters as they were walking alongside the road coming home. They were boys from the Duncan sawmill family over in Duncanville. Mama and Pa knew the boys' parents.

The incident happened when my sisters were in sight of our house and Pa was on the front porch. He saw it with his own eyes. The boy driving aimed the car at my sisters like he was going to run over them. Then, just as he was inches away from hitting them, he turned sharply back onto the road. Seeing my sisters scuffling to get out of the way and falling in the ditch, the boys all laughed themselves silly as they drove on down the road.

Pa knew it was just a matter of time before they'd have to come back along that same road. And a couple of hours later when they did, he got himself a big stick and stood in the middle of the road holding this stick up and he stopped the T-Model Ford dead in its tracks.

He told those white boys that he'd beat the living mess out of them if they ever pulled a trick like that again. They turned red and apologized to Pa and promised never to do it again. He then stepped aside and let them go.

The only time Pa got seriously crabby was when he felt underpaid, or didn't get paid at all for a building job he'd done for somebody. He always did quality work, such as building the first post office Dublinville ever had. Before that, people picked up mail at the general store. Pa also put up the first doctors' office building in town. Before that, doctors, all white, had their offices in their homes. There were no black doctors in Dublinville. Pa was also one of the builders selected to help build Stone Mountain resort in the 1920s.

But some of those white folks wouldn't pay him what he deserved when he did carpentry or house construction work for them, and that made him angry. They'd promise one thing, then, when he'd finish the job, they'd make up some excuse to pay less or nothing.

Despite the fact that the days of slavery were long past, some white folks thought nothing of taking advantage of a colored man and the work he did for them. Some still believed Negro labor should be free to white folks because they knew only white privilege. It was the way they were brought up. You could say they couldn't imagine any other way of living. On the other hand, some white folks were just downright dishonest and unprincipled. When Pa was unhappy, I was unhappy. I disliked anything that made him unhappy.

Some white folk didn't like to see a man like Pa with the kind of skill he had. It looked uppity to them. All the time we heard stories about white folks misusing colored folks. A colored friend of Pa's in Athens, a skilled blacksmith, was fired so an untrained white man could go to work in his place as a trainee. Whenever a white man could do another white man a favor, and if a black man was in the way, the black man got the ax. Most white folks in our town thought there was a natural relationship between black people and poverty. And they wanted to keep it that way.

It was not unusual for Pa to build somebody a house and after paying off his workers end up with only a hundred dollars clear for himself. That kind of thing insulted Pa's intelligence and goodwill.

But despite these problems with money, we were among the better off colored folk, even if a lot of that was just appearance. Some white people who didn't have the money—or said they didn't have it—paid Pa with things. That's how we came to be the only colored family in town with fine antique furniture in every room. Sometimes the furniture had been passed down for generations in a family before it ended up in Pa's hands. We never could have afforded those things any other way. But more than antiques, what we often needed was the money Pa wasn't getting.

Anyway, Pa had good credit at all the stores in town. When I was little, I loved bananas and I used to just stop in the grocery store and pick out a banana and sign Pa's name and be on my way. All of the Hull kids could do that. All the shopkeepers knew us to be Pa's children and they knew he was good for the money.

When he was on a job putting up, say, a new porch or a new banister somewhere, I would go with one of my older sisters to take him his lunch. Usually the houses were in or near town, and I enjoyed the adventure. On the way back home we'd pick up the mail and stop in the grocery store and buy some candy or whatever on Pa's credit.

Pa never whipped us children. Once Bert took Pa's hunting rifle out of the house without permission and showed it to one of the Hull cousins, and Pa caught him in the backyard. There was a strict rule—none of the children were supposed to play with the rifle. But it wasn't Pa himself who gave Bert a butt whipping. It was Mama. She tore up his behind. But that was the only time.

One day—I was eleven then—I overheard Pa and Mama talking about the banks being broke. Not wanting me to hear the rest of the conversation, they told me to go outside and play. Out on the porch Saffrey said that Pa and Mama were upset because the banks were broke. I said that ain't nothing, Pa can fix the banks just like he fixes everything else.

Pa was born William Henry Hicks on July 12, 1868, in Wilkes County, Georgia. As I said earlier, his mother, Melanie—Nee for short—had been a slave before he was born. Her name was Lowella Melanie (1835–1903) and she, as a young girl, had been bought in

Virginia by Judge Rory Hicks and brought back to Wilkes County, where Hicks was the judge at the courthouse. I mentioned earlier the family ties to Virginia.

Before the Civil War the Hicks were a prominent white Georgia family, with six boys and three girls. All the boys were pretty well educated. Two or three of them were educated in law and the others became farmers. The girls all married farmers.

Before the war the family had a reputation among other white folks for treating their slaves just like their own children. This was a sly way of acknowledging that some of them were actually blood relatives. One of Judge Rory Hicks's lawyer brothers for a while also got himself elected to some sort of public office, and I've heard that he was a fine public speaker.

Also, I've been told that the old Wilkes County courthouse was on the north side of the square, and it was well known as the site of Confederate cabinet meetings near the end of the Civil War.

Years later, Nee married a man named Hull and gave Pa that man's name. Although Judge Hicks was Pa's flesh-and-blood father, Pa gave up the name Hicks and became legally Hull's son. Everybody knew this sort of thing—white men being the blood father and black men being the legal father—was common up and down the old slave states.

Pa grew up in Judge Hicks's home, where his mother stayed on after Emancipation as head of the servants and a companion to the old man. While living in his father's house, Pa had a tutor who came to the house and taught him Latin, arithmetic, reading and writing. It was said that the tutor was a foreigner, maybe Italian.

The judge told everybody that he didn't want his son in any Negro normal school. The tutor also taught the boy the basics for planning and constructing and building houses. And Pa read a lot, too, about blueprint making and such things.

After his mother married, Pa moved to Dublinville to live with his mother and his stepfather. He was nearly forty, a bit old to be still living with his father, then later with his mother. One of the judge's sisters, pa's Aunt Saffrey—my sister was named after her—used to come up to Dublinville to see about Pa after he moved.

She came in a fancy horse-drawn buggy. And she'd pull up to the Hull house and stop and Pa would come outside. Curious neighbors leaned out windows watching her talking with Pa. By then Pa had half-sisters and half-brothers, but I never knew how many because there were so many of them.

In fact, Pa was living with his mother when Mama met him. Mama was eighteen years younger than Pa. The first time she ever saw Pa was just before he moved out of his father's house and just after the old judge's death.

Pa was sitting up in a fancy carriage drawn by four horses. This carriage had tassels all around it and to her, Pa himself looked like a million dollars. He was coming up from Wilkes County to see Nee in Dublinville.

And when Mama saw this handsome man driving those pretty horses, she said she was really impressed. Mama was about seventeen at the time. She was living in Atlanta with her cousin Gussie, and working for a white lady, Mrs. Silverstone, caring for her son, and attending classes at the Negro normal school, Spelman. Mama was back in Dublinville just for a visit.

Pa was smitten. The sight of her was all it took. Having lived in the big city, she appeared to Pa to be more polished than the other girls in Dublinville did. Not many young colored women her age owned their own sewing machines. And she was good-looking, too. So they took to each other right away.

After Judge Hicks died and Pa was living in Dublinville, he and Mama kept noticing each other in church and around town. At some point they must have started courting in a polite mannerly way—in the way people in the country did their romancing—in a shy and what was thought a proper manner.

They married on Mama's twentieth birthday—June 29, 1906. And the first house they lived in was close to the railroad tracks and up the hill by the white folks' cemetery. It was just off the road that came down into town.

So now that Pa was married and living in Dublinville, and he had all of these half-sisters and half-brothers around, he came to know them better and to know his stepfather, Slim Hull, too.

I wasn't old enough to keep a lot of names straight

when all the Hull children were around, so I never really knew them by name. And then they started having children of their own, which meant more names. Like I said, there were so many of them.

And I never had a clear memory of their daddy Mr. Slim Hull himself, but I remember one of his daughters or granddaughters. By then, to my way of seeing, she was a grown woman who lived in a one-room shack with a brick chimney.

She had an iron rod going across her fireplace. On that rod she hung pots and did her cooking. Some white boys once tried to scare her by dropping a rabbit down her chimney. She just told everybody the Devil may have brought the rabbit, but God sent it.

Mama herself was born Ada Mae Bronner on June 29, 1886, in Oglethorpe County out in the country away from any city or town. She had twelve sisters and brothers. Her mother, Grandma Lucy Dupree (born 1852), was married three times, to George Mills in 1869, to Fred Franklin in 1891, and to Burley Bronner in 1896. And I didn't know anything about her first two husbands. Mama's father, Burley "Bibb" Bronner (born 1848), was Lucy's third husband.

As a girl, Mama learned to do a lot, and became a very independent person. She later earned her own money by making soap and blankets and dresses. She also was an expert at cooking fancy and plain dishes. Her mother had taught her how to be self-reliant.

I got to know Grandma Lucy Mills well because

she came to visit a lot. When I was born she came to help Mama with me just as she'd come to help with each of the others at birth. As the last of Mama's children, Grandma Lucy gave me her bowl and pitcher set. It was used for bathing all Mama's children when we were infants.

I liked Grandma Lucy all right, but she was strict. One time when she and Mama were back in the kitchen, I came in and asked for a penny to go get some candy. Grandma snapped a *no* at me and told me to go on back outside and play. Instead, I ran up to the living room and patted my butt at her picture hanging on the wall. I must have done that a few times when she made me mad.

My grandfather, Bibb Bronner, was two-thirds Cherokee Indian. I remembered him well, too. He was a small dark man with straight hair, a straight nose, and high cheekbones. He went to town every Saturday morning, taking with him brooms for sale that he himself made. He also kept bees and gathered the honey. He sold the honey, in jars, also at the Saturday market. He was not a talker. I didn't get to know him well. I don't think anybody except Grandma Lucy did.

Four

One time, Mama, Bert, Saffrey, a friend of Mama's, Frances Gillipan, and I drove over to Clarke County in Pa's new Chevrolet to visit Aunt Georgia Mills, Mama's oldest sister. Her legs had just been amputated. I didn't remember why. Probably diabetes.

Bert drove us there, but during the long afternoon we spent visiting, he got in with the young men around there and drank some corn whiskey and got drunk as a skunk. This was the winter I was eleven, and the stock market had just crashed. Everybody was talking about it.

Aunt Georgia's family owned milk cows, and before we left she loaded Mama down with milk and butter. Mama tried to be polite and not take so much, but finally she gave in and took all that she was offered. Then we gave our kisses and said our good-byes. We helped Mama load all the milk and butter into the car.

Although snow was unusual in Georgia even in the

winter, on the way back it was snowing heavily and it was pitch-dark. Saffrey was in the front with Bert, who was again driving—but shouldn't have been— and they were arguing about his driving.

Saffrey was sixteen and wanted the steering wheel—despite the fact that she didn't trust her own driving—but he wouldn't give it up. Worried about Bert's driving, she kept trying to yank it from him, making the car zigzag. I was in the back with Frances and Mama. And I was worried about Bert's driving, too.

Then he lost control of the car—drove it over an embankment into a sewage ditch. I went through the windshield. Mama's top lip was cut off. The steering wheel broke in Bert's mouth and knocked out all of his front teeth. Saffrey's knee was gashed to the bone. Frances was bleeding. And the doors were still closed.

After a while, two other cars came by and stopped. I remember a lot of white people with flashlights coming down the embankment to see about us. I was the only one outside the car when they got there, outside because being so small, I had gone through the windshield. I was just standing there and probably in shock. It was amazing, but I was hurt less than anybody. Oh, I was cut on the forehead, but not badly.

On a Sunday afternoon four decades later, I had occasion to visit Bradley, Illinois, and on the way back to the train station, the left front wheel of the taxi flew off. The car swerved, dipped, bounced and shot off the road. It bounced again, then plunged down an embankment. It came to rest in an open field.

I pushed myself up off the floor and looked around, and saw the driver shaking his head, trying to get his senses back. I didn't see any blood on him. Then the back door opened, and two boys and two girls were looking in at me. Are you all right? I think so, I said.

They were students from Bradley University, where my youngest daughter, Cassandra, was in her second year. Others were helping the driver out. He seemed to be fine. Lucky for us the car hadn't turned over. And I remembered that time when Bert ran off the road and wrecked Pa's car, and almost killed us all. But this time I was all right. Not a scar, not a bruise. I felt fine.

For some reason I kept saying, my train is leaving in ten minutes. And the Bradley students put me in their car and rushed me to the station. They escorted me right up to the train and saw that I got on safely. One boy brought my overnight bag and set it on my lap just as the train was pulling out. He waved good-bye and jumped off. And I thought to myself, Sometimes people can be good, especially when it really counts.

The people with the flashlights worked long and hard at getting the car doors opened. Then they finally helped Mama, Bert, Frances and Saffrey out. They were covered with blood, butter and milk. They looked worse than they were. And Mama cried out, Lord! Look at all of my good milk and butter gone to waste.

These people put Saffrey and Bert in the first car, then Mama, Frances and me in the second car. They drove us to the nearest town, Crawford, to a doctor's house.

We waited while one of them knocked on the doctor's door and got him up out of his bed. The front porch light went on. The doctor and his wife both came out to the porch. His office was the front room of his house. Turning on lights inside, they led us into his office.

It must, by then, have been two in the morning. The doctor told his wife to bring him lots of warm water. Three or four of the people who'd brought us there went with her to help. He needed to clean our wounds and clean the glass off our skin. They brought back four shallow pans of hot water and placed them on his examination table. Then we thanked the kind people who'd helped us. They said it was nothing and left. We heard them drive off.

After we were clean, the doctor and his wife medicated our cuts and sewed us up. They put three or four stitches in my temples and sewed Mama's lip back on. They gave Bert some painkilling drug for his mouth. His teeth were broken off to the gums and he was in a lot of pain. Saffrey and Frances were bandaged up.

Scroll forward in time to September 1983. Saffrey called me in Chicago and said, Inez, Bert has been shot to death. He was found dead. This news hit me hard. I hadn't felt as close to Bert as I had to my sisters and my other brother, Wilbur. I felt a sudden sense of painful, bitter loss, especially since Bert had never allowed anybody to get close to him. He rebuffed all expressions of tenderness. I didn't believe he felt tenderly toward anybody but Mama.

I flew home in a hurry.

At the house, sitting on the front porch, was one of Bert's longtime friends and fellow church members, a carpenter, like Bert.

He said, The funeral already started, but you can probably make it before it ends. The preacher gonna talk a long time, he said I know that for a fact.

I got to the church just as the pallbearers were carrying Bert's coffin out through the back door to the little graveyard that stretched from the side to the rear. The congregation followed. The pallbearers put Bert down into the ground behind the church. Mama's grave was on the side. All the while, Brenna was screaming at the top of her voice, Oh, Lord, why did they have to kill my brother? Why? Why?

When the burial was over and we were back at the house, everybody told us that Sheriff Pete Kraft booked the death as suicide. I couldn't believe my ears. My brother committed suicide? No way. Saffrey said, Bert didn't know nothing about no suicide. We were all shaking our heads in disbelief. And Brenna was still saying, Why, why did they have to kill him? He never bothered anybody. Why?

❧

My brother was grandfather to Tom, Nealy's son. We all called him Tank. And a little later I said, Tank, show me where you found your grandpa's body. And he took me outside and across the backyard to the old rock shed we called the toolhouse. Tank pointed to the spot by the shed where Bert was supposed to have shot himself.

Tank said, The shotgun was propped against the wall right there. Granddaddy was lying right here. Tank touched the spot with his shoe toe. I said, Now, you mean to tell me Sheriff Kraft wants us to believe that Bert shot himself in the stomach with a shotgun, then took the time to prop the shotgun back upside this wall? Tank said, That's what he's saying. And Tank grinned. I said, Do you believe he shot himself? I watched Tank closely. And Tank scratched his head, and looking away to the side, he said, Yeah, I believe he shot himself.

The next morning I went to see Sheriff Pete Kraft. He was at his desk when I walked in. He knew me, so I didn't have to tell him who I was. He was a little, round pink man with a bald head and a cigar at the corner of his mouth. I said, Sheriff, I come to see how your investigation of my brother's death is going.

He blinked a few times and stuttered, then said, There ain't no investigation. It's finished, Inez. Nealy called me. That's how I found out. Nealy called and said, Sheriff, Bert done committed suicide. She said her son, Tank, found the body. He and a white man together. So that was good enough for me, having the white man there and everything, I took Tank's word, said Sheriff Kraft.

Then I said, So you're just going to take Nealy's word that it was suicide? And he said, Inez, we don't investigate when we know how a person died. Then I said, I want this death investigated, Sheriff. Bert's arm wasn't long enough to have pulled the trigger of that shotgun, and aim it at his own stomach at the same time. He leaned back in his chair and chewed his cigar and said, I don't know if we'd find anything, Inez. What's the point? Besides, Bert used a stick with a string on it. That's how he did it.

I just looked at Sheriff Kraft. I didn't believe a word of it. He was trying to tell me my brother pulled the trigger of a shotgun with a string tied to a stick, and after shooting himself in the stomach, he propped the shotgun against the toolhouse. The stick and the string made no sense. The propped-up shotgun made no sense. It was a cock-and-bull story if I ever heard one.

So I left Sheriff Kraft chewing his cigar. I walked outside and ran smack dead into Mr. Tinsley. We apologized at the same time, then we greeted each other. I asked about Miss Christy, his wife. She was fine. Then I said, Tell me what happened to my brother. Mr. Tinsley pushed his hat back on his head and scratched his thin white hair. He said, Bert was out on the front porch and said good morning to me when I went by, but I didn't see him any more that day. That's all I know, Inez.

Later, back at the house, I asked more questions of neighbors, then questioned Arlene, Nealy and Tank again. And I learned that Arlene had called Mama's house around dinnertime to tell Bert to come home to eat. He was at Mama's at his usual time to check on the house. Arlene knew he was supposed to be there, so she kept trying. When finally she got no answer, she told her daughter, Nealy, she'd be right back and she drove down there. She found Bert's truck parked in the back-yard. His door keys were stuck in the back door lock.

After a while, she drove back home, not knowing what to think. Every hour or so, for the rest of the night, she called and got no answer. In the morning, she sent Tank to see what he could find out. Tank stopped at the bus station across the street and somehow a white man ended up going to the house with Tank.

It was the white man who found the body. I didn't know the white man's name. But I thought his finding Bert's body was interesting. He was just one of those country white men who sat in front of the bus station most of the day.

Next thing I did was pay the coroner a visit. I could see that she wasn't happy to see me. I told her about the stick theory. Then I said, Why didn't you take the stick with the string when you took the body? I never saw any stick with a string, she said. Who said there was a stick? His grandson, Tank, I said. But I could see from her expression that I was getting nowhere by talking with her.

It was clear that she didn't want to hear anymore. On the way back to the house, I kept puzzling over Bert's death. No one yet had offered an explanation as to how the stick walked by itself from the toolhouse area to the back porch after Bert was already down. That was where Tank said he found the stick and string. How, then, did he know Bert had used the device on the shotgun?

The next day I went to the courthouse and formally ordered a hearing on Bert's death. And they set a date a month away. I couldn't stay in Dublinville that long, so I flew back home. But when I got there all I could think about was the horrible way my brother must have died. For days, I stayed on the phone talking with Wilbur, Saffrey and Brenna. We tried as best we could to comfort each other.

We searched our minds for answers. Could Bert have really killed himself? He was a deacon and treasurer of the church. We'd never known any church people to ever do such a thing. Nealy, at one point, said, Daddy had cancer. Cancer? I called and spoke with Bert's doctor and he said, No, Bert didn't have cancer. He was in pretty good health, for his age.

After the hearing, Nealy called me and said, Aunt Inez, the hearing did not prove suicide. She said that the conclusion of the court was "inconclusive." The authorities believed that there was not enough evidence pointing in any direction to go after a murderer. But that was not my belief. And day by day, anger was building in my bosom.

I had a gut feeling about this thing. I knew Bert didn't

kill himself. It just didn't fit. But I was making myself sick with anger. Plus none of us—Wilbur or Saffrey or Brenna—had the money to sponsor our own investigation.

When the doctor in Crawford finished fixing us up, we thanked him and his wife, and the doctor himself drove us home in his car. I thought, What great kindness! on the part of those people who helped us! What great kindness! on the part of that doctor and his wife, who put us back together.

When we got home, somehow Pa already knew about the accident. Maybe one of the people who'd helped us had stopped by and told him. I never really knew how he found out ahead of time, but I do know that he never bought another car after that one was destroyed. And Bert didn't get a chance to drive another car till he was able to buy himself one.

Five

I met Clarence when I was sixteen. I was still a student at Union in Athens when he drove the brother of one of my classmates from Atlanta for a visit. That's when Clarence first saw me. I say it like that because I think he saw me before I noticed him.

He seemed nice enough but I was not especially attracted to him. He was ten years older than I was. When I told him where I lived, he smiled and said his mother, Miss Anna, lived in Dublinville. I said I didn't know her. And he said, Don't worry, you will.

Before going home in May—having completely forgotten about Clarence—I signed up as an agent with Stone Mountain Afra-Mutual, a colored insurance company in Athens, to sell policies to colored people in and around Dublinville. I knew where all the colored people lived and it was just a matter of walking around and knocking on doors. I was excited about my job, and I set out to build a route for the company.

One day I knocked at the door of a two-room frame house I knew to be colored and a heavy-set *white* woman opened the door. I thought I'd made a mistake. I apologized and explained that I was selling insurance to colored people.

The woman gave me a big friendly smile and invited me in. She told me to make myself at home. When she did that, I suspected she was like me—colored but didn't look it. But how come I didn't know her? I introduced myself and she said, People call me Miss Anna.

This Miss Anna was to become an important person in my life. She was the mother of the man I would later marry, the man to whom I gave my virginity, the father of my first two children.

She said she was new in town. Certainly new to me. She'd lived in Dublinville once before, moved away, and was here again. Then I remembered that man in Athens—Clarence somebody—telling me his mother lived in Dublinville. So this was his mother, Miss Anna. I told her I'd recently met her son in Athens at one of the games.

This is what she told me. Originally from Oglethorpe County, Miss Anna, in recent years, had been on the move, traveling and preaching, but was settled in Dublinville for the time being. She also worked as a housekeeper or a cook. She was currently cooking full-time for a Dublinville family.

Since her children were now all grown and gone, she was free to travel as a part-time preacher, going from town to town in Georgia and Tennessee and

Alabama, speaking as a guest in churches. But right now she was tired of doing that.

All the grown-ups in Dublinville back then knew parts of Miss Anna's story, but only parts.

Miss Anna's white mother, Rebecca Lankford was the daughter of Curtis Caldwell Lankford and Nancy A. E. McCarty Lankford, both uneducated farm workers. They had four boys and two girls. Rebecca was born in 1858.

Her father, Curtis, was born in 1827 in Jackson County, Georgia. Having enlisted in April 1861 at Augusta, he served as a private in Company C, Third Regiment, Georgia Infantry, in the Confederate Army during the Civil War for one year. Discharged early because of rheumatism contracted from having to sleep on the ground, Curtis was not present when his company surrendered in April 1865 at Appomattox, Virginia. He died in June 1887.

Rebecca's mother, Nancy McCarty, was also born in Jackson County, in 1832, and was living with her father, John, and her mother, Anna, a year before her marriage to Curtis. After many years of also suffering with rheumatism and being cared for by her children, she died around 1920.

Rebecca's grandfather, John McCarty Sr., was a descendant of Cornelius McCarty, who'd come over from Ireland sometime before 1775. He served in the South Carolina militia that year. In 1779 he lent South Carolina forty thousand dollars in the then present-day currency. A lot of money! He died in

August 1782. Meanwhile his son Daniel was in Lincoln County, North Carolina, in March 1777 and fought under Captain Hambright against the Cherokee Indians. Davy Crockett was living in Lincoln County, too, at the time, and he and Daniel were probably acquainted.

Rebecca gave birth to a daughter on May 5, 1878, in Oglethorpe County. She named her Anna after her own grandmother, Nancy's mother. On June 27 she charged a young white man, William T. Bowling, with "bastardy," accusing him of being the father of her child. The real father of her child was Stephen Bowling, a black man, son of Harriet Bowling, a former slave on the Bowling Plantation. Charging William rather than Stephen may have been Rebecca's way of protecting Stephen from a lynch mob. Anyway, the charges were not sustained. Both William and Stephen married other women a short time later.

When Anna was not yet a year old Rebecca gave her away to a colored lady, Edith Jackson (1858–1933), who also had just had a baby, Irene, whom she was nursing. Rebecca never told any white folks who the father was. Stephen Bowling would have been lynched on the spot. Few black men who ever touched a white woman lived to tell about it. But there were some colored folks, of course, who knew and never told anybody till years later when Anna was a big girl. White folks took such things seriously, especially after the Civil War. We all knew that. It was one of the first things we learned as children.

According to family legend, when Rebecca dropped off little Anna at Edith Jackson's, she said, Now listen here, Edith, don't you be letting my baby suck from the same titty you got yours sucking from. Keep them apart. You hear? Every colored person in Dublinville knew that story, and some thought it was funny. Others thought it was crazy. It just showed—as funny as it was—that even Rebecca, who loved a black man, was not foolish enough to give up the privilege that came with being identified as white.

In February 1887, when Anna was almost nine, her maternal grandmother, Harriet Bowling, adopted her and raised her. In the adoption papers Anna was identified as Rebecca's. At this point she was called Re[becca] Talbot. She was said to be no longer living. A short time after giving up her baby she probably married a man named Talbot.

When I met her, Miss Anna had already married three times, the last time to George Major, Clarence's father. She was now divorced.

That was Miss Anna's background. This was now. Miss Anna was cooking for Edward Webster, my birth father's brother. So she was in his house every day. And Clarence would often drive from Atlanta to visit his mother. That was how we started seeing each other on a regular basis.

Whenever he was in Dublinville on these trips, he'd drive his mother down to see Mama. And while Mama and Miss Anna were back in the kitchen talking, Clarence and I sat in the swing on the front porch and talked. We were not at the holding-hands stage. Just talking. He asked me a lot of questions about myself, about school and about my insurance work. I was beginning to like him. He was gentle. He seemed interested in me as a person.

I was also at that time helping Ogden Jackson out with the smaller children at the Harriet Beecher Stowe School. I taught them their ABCs and numbers. Their regular teacher—his mother, Miss Bessy Jackson—had just had surgery. In fact, I was sweet on Ogden and I thought he liked me, too. But neither one of us ever took the step.

I could tell that Clarence was not pleased when I talked about Ogden. Yet Clarence wanted to know all about my experiences at Stowe School, too. I talked and talked about what I was doing, but he never said anything about himself. And I guess I didn't pry beyond once saying, So you live and work in Atlanta? But he didn't take the bait.

Then one day while I was sitting in the swing with Clarence, he handed me an expensive fountain pen and said, Since you're filling out insurance forms for people, I thought you needed a nice pen to write with. Surprised, I took the pen and uncapped it. It was beautiful, silver and gold.

But I didn't feel that I could take such an expensive gift from a person I hardly knew. And I told him so. He just laughed. Then I offered to pay him for it, but he said, No. Someday you're going to be my wife. You don't need to pay me. And we both laughed about that. It seemed so out of the question. At least to me it did.

In the meantime, I had signed up a lot of people for insurance. It was also my job to go around and collect payments. I then sent the money on to Athens. But the company was in the process of setting up a system by which customers could mail in their payments. Given this developing situation, I figured I'd be better off going to Atlanta, the big city, and finding a job. I had no prospects in Dublinville.

One day—just before it was time for Clarence to drive his mother back home—I happened to mention that I would be moving to Atlanta. I was excited about moving back to the city. I said, I have to find myself a job. I'd like to continue selling insurance. I want to be independent, but in the meantime, I'll be staying with my brother, Wilbur, and his wife, Carrie. Clarence smiled and said, Good, I'll see you then. What made him so sure? Could his self-confidence have had such an overpowering effect on me? Was it what later caused me to surrender so completely to his will? Surely my youth and inexperience had something to do my response to him.

I was going on seventeen now, and I had started dressing in a more grown-up manner, and wearing makeup. The minute I got to Wilbur's house, Carrie told me that Clarence had been by there a few days earlier and told her that he was going to marry me. I laughed. To my sister-in-law I said, I'm not thinking about marrying anybody, Carrie. You know that.

Clarence came to the house a week later. I wasn't afraid of spending time with him. I thought I could enjoy his company without sharing his plans. I was so young and innocent that I wasn't even aware of how completely I lost myself in his presence. What little hesitation in myself that I was conscious of I ignored completely.

For two weeks he and I had a great time together—going to the movies and eating out and visiting small towns on the outskirts of Atlanta. He was charming and kind to me. And he was good to look at—always dressed in silk shirts and expensive slacks and highly polished shoes. I liked his dimples when he smiled. His hands were soft, so I knew he didn't do manual labor. I began to fear that I was enjoying his company too much. Who was this man? He was too good to be true, yet I kept seeing him—in a proper and polite way, of course.

Then one Saturday, on the way back from a movie, we stopped at a pawnshop. I want to show you something, he said. And to my surprise, we looked at wedding rings. He pointed to the most expensive ones in the showcase and asked me which rings I liked best. I was stunned. I had no idea what to say. I was puzzled. Here he was showing me wedding rings and hadn't yet asked me if I'd marry him. I had a romantic sense of how courtship should lead to marriage. And this was not the way. Besides, I wasn't interested in marrying.

Although I hesitated now for sure, and was conscious of it, I pointed to the ring I liked best, telling myself that he was only asking about my taste in jewelry.

It was widely rumored that Clarence ran a gambling business in Buttermilk Bottom. A few days after the pawnshop incident, Carrie told me she'd heard another rumor, circulated up from Buttermilk Bottom, that he was already engaged to some woman down there. Both rumors bothered me. I didn't want to be involved with a gambler, and I certainly didn't want to be dating a man who was engaged to another woman.

But I liked Clarence, liked him more and more—not that I knew anything about him. He certainly seemed better off than most of the other colored men I knew. Whenever I'd tried to get him to tell me about himself, about his work, he'd say a few words that didn't add up to much, and shift the talk back to me by asking me about something I was doing.

Finally, I got brave. I said, Clarence, why don't you tell me exactly what kind of work you do? He blinked, then smiled and said, I own a gambling establishment down in Buttermilk Bottom. I wasn't surprised to hear this. Rumors had a way of containing some truth. I wasn't happy about the news, yet I liked him, so I wasn't ready to stop seeing him because of the gambling, although in my family, gambling was considered one of the worst things a person could do. Pa would have said it was immoral.

But I let the gambling slide. I said, I've heard that you have a girlfriend down there that you're engaged to marry. Is that true? Clarence smiled and shook his head. People talk all the time, he said, you can't believe everything you hear. There's nothing to that rumor.

At the same time, Carrie took me aside and told me that she thought it was a good idea for me to marry Clarence. She said he was a good man. He paid rent for people who couldn't pay their own. He bought food for the hungry. He was good to all the children. In the neighborhood he was always helping friends and strangers. Carrie said everybody knew him and a lot of people depended on his good will. She felt that I couldn't go wrong with him.

I absorbed Carrie's message. Clarence had been very kind to me. So, I too, thought he was a good person. The next time he showed up he said, I have something to show you, but you have to come with me to see it. He then drove us over to a house on McGruder, a sloping, irregular street. It was about a twenty-minute walk from Five Points, the Negro business district at Decatur and Marietta, Whitehall and Peachtree.

The house was on the corner, and it was a plain, unpainted, wood-frame house with a four-step wooden stairway up to the porch, like all the others along that hilly street. The house itself was perched on brick columns to guard against flooding. Clarence opened the door to a fully furnished place. I was surprised, but I shouldn't have been. I wondered if this man's self-confidence knew no end.

His sister Minnie was there, standing on a chair backed up to a window. Minnie turned around from hanging bright yellow curtains and greeted me with a big smile and dimples. The whole family had dimples. I'd met Minnie just recently through Clarence. Seven years older than me, she was nice. And I liked her— then and always. Minnie said, You like your new place?

There was all of this preparation, and Clarence still hadn't asked me to marry him. Yet two days later, he, Minnie and I drove down to Decatur and got the license I felt lulled into the trip He had come in and said, Get ready, Minnie is going to be our witness, we're going to get the license. He was incredibly persuasive. I'd never known anyone like him.

No doubt about it, part of me was happy, even excited by the prospect of marriage. I couldn't think of any good reason to say, No, I can't do this. Yet part of me now clearly was not comfortable with the way he was going about the transition from courtship to covenant. Yet the fact that he was ten years older than I was probably in part caused me to follow his instructions without much question.

The next day a neighbor came by and told me that there was a notice in the newspaper that we'd applied for a marriage license. I should have known the announcement would be in the paper, but I didn't. It hadn't crossed my mind. I began to worry. I hadn't told Wilbur, nor Pa or Mama. I was afraid they'd disapprove. Some part of me was driven to marry Clarence. And now I wanted to hurry and get it done before my brother or father stopped me. Carrie was my collaborator.

Clarence found a preacher, a Reverend Roberts, a man with bushy sideburns. He was a friend of Clarence's. The minister, in a three-piece suit, came to the house on McGruder Street, carrying a Bible and his little black marriage book. Already dressed up and waiting for him, we stood before him. Minnie and a neighbor woman were standing to the side as witnesses.

Reverend Roberts said, Repeat after me. Clarence and I repeated the marriage vows, word for word, after the preacher. They were the usual words, nothing unusual, yet the moment carried a lot of magic for me. Something important was happening in my life. Perhaps it was one of the most important things up to that point. Yet I ignored that part of myself that disliked the fact that this ceremony was not in a church. That was the way my family would have wanted it. I ignored that part of myself that felt cheated out of a grand place of light and music. I refused to think about a gathering of lots of people celebrating the magic I felt. I ignored my dislike for the darkness of the house in which we stood repeating a man's words, ignored my fear of what I was doing.

Carrie told Wilbur after the marriage ceremony was behind us. When Clarence and I went to pick up my clothes, Carrie said that my brother was upset. Then Wilbur himself walked in as we were gathering my things—and did he perform! He told Clarence off. Wilbur finally said, You're too old for this girl, she's just an innocent child. She don't know what she's getting herself into. You know better. And if I ever hear tell of you mistreating her, I'm coming after you myself. You got that, Clarence? Clarence shook his head, trying to look sympathetic to Wilbur's feelings.

The last thing Wilbur said was to me, though. He said, If he don't treat you right, come right back here, where you belong. He said this in front of Clarence, who was very smart to keep quiet.

But Wilbur didn't stay mad long. He and Clarence went on being friends after the telling off. Clarence said it was just something Wilbur had to do, being my oldest brother. But Wilbur himself later told me that he hoped he was wrong about Clarence. He wanted me to be happy. He was going to pray that things worked out for me. He said he liked Clarence, but not as my husband. Maybe he would get used to the idea. After all, like it or not, Clarence was now his brother-in-law.

A few days after Wilbur's angry outburst, I went to work at the Piedmont Hotel as an elevator operator. The Piedmont was downtown, and it was one of the two largest and best hotels in Atlanta. They hired only yellow girls—that's what they called us—to work the elevators, yellow girls and white boys. White girls worked the front desk and the office. It was unusual, but the yellow girls and white girls shared the same locker room. And this was at a time when the South was rigidly segregated. Black and white people were forced by law to use separate public facilities of every kind.

Unlike most other men, Clarence didn't mind his wife working. In fact, he thought it was great that I wanted to earn my own money. His attitude was a pleasant surprise. But I shouldn't have been surprised. Nothing about Clarence was average.

The hotel ran three shifts, and they already worked two other girls. I was hired as a swing-shift girl, which meant that I had to work a lot of different shifts with all kinds of unpredictable hours.

I worked the morning and afternoon and night shifts, any shift of any girl who took off. The white boy, Billy Roe, who was training me was a very happy boy, and I liked him because he was easygoing and I could tell he liked me a lot. He was so happy to be getting his blue bellhop suit. He reasoned that dressed in that pretty new suit, he would make bigger tips.

Clarence's sister Minnie was now living with us. And she had one of those everyday domestic jobs, cooking and cleaning house for a young white couple. Although all three of my sisters, from time to time, did that kind of work, it was a type of work I myself somehow never did—not that I felt above it, it was just something that never occurred to me to do. And it was good to have Minnie around. She and I got along fine. We even wore each other's clothes.

After the marriage, Clarence was spending a lot of time in Buttermilk Bottom with his gambling business. He usually got home late or didn't come home till daybreak when the gambling ended. And now that I was married to him, I learned that he not only ran the gambling business but controlled the numbers routes, too.

In the meantime, Minnie met a fellow she liked, and she moved out to be with him in his place. But she came by often. So now, every day I was coming home to an empty house. I missed Minnie. I didn't like having to be alone so often. The fact that I had made friends with a few of my neighbors didn't help much. I was more depressed by the way things were turning out so soon than I allowed myself to admit.

I'd been on the job about two months when it happened. I went to work one payday with the intention of running the elevator as usual. Instead of putting on my uniform and going to work, I walked into my boss's office. We exchanged greetings. I picked up my paycheck, and was about to leave when I turned to him. Without having planned to do so, I told Mr. Paxton that I was going to be off for a while. I hadn't known I was going to say that.

The words just came out. I said that I was going to see my mother and father. And tears started streaming down my cheeks. I had been trying to ignore it, to deny it, but there it was. The fact was, I was miserable. While I sobbed, Mr. Paxton tried to comfort me, and I thanked him. Then I took my check and said good-bye.

I wrote Clarence a note and left it on the table. And on my way to the bus station, I stopped by Carrie's and told her where I was going. I had already let Minnie know, and she said, He is so selfish. You're doing the right thing, Nez. Leaving might wake him up.

I had written to Pa and Mama about my marriage, and Mama wrote back saying that they were disappointed, but wished me the best. Both said they wished I had waited and gotten more education. They wanted me to establish myself as a self-supporting woman. Mama strongly believed in women being self-sufficient.

But when I arrived home, ironically, it was Pa who seemed most disappointed by my marriage. And the fact that I was already back home just proved to him how right he was. All I could do was hang my head and keep silent, hoping his anger would pass quickly.

After a few days at Mama's, I started to get sick to the stomach. I couldn't keep food down. So Mama sent for a doctor to come to the house. He looked at me with his blue eyes and said, Ada, she might be pregnant. The doctor gave me something to take, and two days later—whatever it was—it made me sicker. I vomited up the medicine *and* my food.

So Mama suggested that I go to Athens to see Dr. Lumpkin, a black doctor she knew. I took the bus there. His office was in a complex of offices with other colored doctors and dentists and optometrists and so on. These doctors all had their own common lab. Dr. Lumpkin had the lab to do a urine test. In a couple of hours, he called me back into his office. Yes, he said, you are very pregnant.

I had very mixed feelings about being pregnant. Something in me responded to the news in a positive way because it felt natural, fulfilling, yet something else, equally strong, met the news with disappointment and sadness.

I took the five o'clock bus back to Dublinville.

About a week later, Clarence and Miss Anna showed up at the door. His mother went on back in the house to talk with Mama, and that left Clarence and me on the front porch, just like in the days when we first met and he was supposed to be courting me.

Again we were sitting in that same swing where he first told me that I would be his wife. I still had deep feelings for him and wanted my marriage to work. I just didn't like the neglect, his constant absence. And I didn't know what to do about it. I hadn't gotten any better at standing up to him and insisting on better treatment.

I told him that I was pregnant and watched his reaction. I could tell he was pleased. He apologized for staying away so much. And he promised to act more like a regular husband. I really want you back home, he said, I miss you, I love you. Your place is home with me. I listened to him and watched his face. He seemed sincere. And to make a long story short, he talked me into coming back. He sparked in me hope for a better relationship. But being pregnant, I also felt a bit trapped. It was not an easy situation.

Later that same day Pa took Clarence aside and told him that he had better keep a big space between his gambling life and me. Pa said that he didn't want to hear of Clarence getting me involved in that kind of life. And Clarence promised Pa that his business and his wife were miles apart. He said they would stay that way, because that was the way he, too, wanted it.

Then after Clarence and his mother drove off, Pa told me that he thought I was a smart girl, but that I hadn't shown good sense in picking a husband. Deep down, part of me knew Pa was right. But I still wasn't paying much attention to that part. I was stubborn that way. And now that I was pregnant it seemed all the more urgent that I do everything in my power to make my marriage work.

I tried to imagine what other man—or what other *type* of man—I might have selected. White men were out of the question. Although I knew that interracial marriages took place up north, they were unheard of in my world. Besides, I was not especially attracted to white men. Yet just about every black man I had ever seen or known, except Pa and Clarence, seemed beaten down.

One of the reasons I'd been attracted to Clarence had to do with the fact that he walked with his head high. Like Pa, he carried himself proudly. What Pa was forgetting was the fact that I didn't *know* men, period. I hadn't picked Clarence. He'd come along and swept me off my feet. And I was too dazzled to say no. I hadn't yet learned how to say no, especially to someone ten years older than myself.

Before Clarence, all I had ever done with a boy was hold hands while walking home from school, or sat on the front porch and talked. There had been only three or four, and they were my own age. Clarence was a man, a grown man, and unlike the boys I'd known, he carried himself like he knew what he was doing. And even with all my doubts now, I was going back to him. Now that I'm married, I kept saying to myself, I want my marriage to work. I told myself that I was no quitter.

Six

According to Minnie and Carrie, Clarence had given up the house on McGruder and rented another one— one side of a duplex—on Nutting Street and Woodrow Place. And if Clarence still stayed out a lot, at least this way I was not far from Carrie and Minnie.

My boss at the Piedmont had meanwhile told me that when I came back to Atlanta, I could have my old job back. He thought I quit in tears like I did because I was unhappy with the swing shift I was stuck on. So he'd promised me that I would have my own shift if I returned. This was good news and an unexpected break. I let him continue to believe what he thought. On the other hand, had a clerk in a store given me too much in change, I would have returned the money.

Clarence, by the way, so far wasn't spending any more time in Buttermilk Bottom. He'd gotten rid of the gambling house. Still, he left every morning dressed in a silk shirt and an expensive suit, like a businessman going to the office. He was also gone sometimes in the evenings, but his absence was nothing like it had been before I left. He seemed sincere in his effort to change.

He left one Friday for Decatur, and came back at midnight that Saturday, with a full moon hanging over Atlanta. He hung his pants on the back of a chair, then came to bed and fell into a deep sleep beside me. In the night, I heard the bedroom window open. In the moonlight, I saw somebody sticking a long pole into the room, lifting Clarence's pants off the back of the chair.

I thought I was dreaming. But I woke enough to see the pants dancing in the air. I jumped up, and in my effort to grab the pants, I fell out of bed, though I managed to grab the pants. Yet I had a hard time pulling the pants from the hook. In attempting to do so, I felt sharp stomach pains. But I saved the pants. And whoever was out there ran away, their shoes crunching gravel as they tore down the alley.

The commotion woke Clarence, and when he saw the shape I was in, fearing we might lose the baby, he rushed me to Grady Hospital. The doctor in the colored ward looked tired and sleepy. He examined me and said I was okay. Then he asked if I worked. When I told him what I did, he said that I shouldn't be working. You are risking a miscarriage, he said. You could well lose the baby from pulling and pushing the elevator door handle all day. Standing on your feet that long is no good. He shook his head.

Clarence said that the would-be thief was somebody who'd followed him from Decatur. But a neighbor lady said no, that it was one of the men who helped Kasper, the bootlegger, with the home brew. The neighbor lady was always sitting in the window at night watching everything that happened on the street. So we never knew for sure who it was. I never knew how much money was in those pants, but Clarence was happy that I had saved them.

I kept on working till I was about six months gone. The day before I quit work, Clarence gave me the money and told me to stop at the real estate office and pay the rent on my way to work. But when I got downtown and was walking by the showcase window of a lady's shop, I saw my reflection.

I was so big that my little brown cloth coat wouldn't cover my stomach. I couldn't even button the coat, and it was unusually cold. So I took the rent money and went in that store and bought myself a new, larger coat—one that I could button. When I told Clarence what I had done, he just laughed, and said, That's all right, you did what you needed to do.

At the beginning of December, the doctor told me that by the end of the month, whether or not I felt pain, I should come to the hospital. And it was near the end of the month—the thirtieth, to be exact—when my water broke. It was just past ten o'clock at night. But there was no pain. Right away, Clarence drove me to the hospital. It was a long delivery, and it was painful, but it was the kind of pain that you soon forget. I named the baby Clarence.

Right after you were born, son, a lot of changes took place. Right in the midst of all of this commotion, Mama came from Dublinville to help me. It was tradition to do so. Miss Claudio Knight moved to Atlanta and, to keep her nanny job, Saffrey moved there, too. I was in the hospital quite a few days. They brought me home in an ambulance with you by my side. They took me in on a stretcher.

I was glad to have Mama there. She spent a month with me, teaching me how to take care of you—how to bathe, burp and feed a baby. Mama washed diapers and cleaned my house. She said, He's a pretty baby, Nez. She sat with me and kept me company. Big Clarence was afraid to pick you up for fear of dropping you. But anyone could see that he was happy to have a son and to be a father. He would goo-goo to you and tickle your toes trying to make you smile. You would not only smile, but laugh, too.

Then, after Mama left, Saffrey and Brenna moved into a house across the street on Nutting. We three sisters were together again now, but grown up. I could look out of my window on the Nutting Street side directly into their front door. That's how close we were. Both sisters helped me a lot with you, especially after Mama left. Even after I was up and about, I was still weak. They washed diapers and helped me clean the house.

You were doing fine so far, and your checkups at the clinic proved to me that you were in good health until one day when you were about two months old. I woke that morning and saw scratches on one side of your face. I knew they were from your fingernails. An infection had set in. The nurses at the clinic treated your face with something, but by the time I got you back home, it was clear that the medication was making the infection worse.

So when I took you back, the doctor decided to admit you to the hospital to treat the inflammation. Every day I took the bus at two o'clock in the afternoon to the hospital to see you. After a few days, I still didn't see any improvement. In fact, one day when I got there, your face was very raw—worse than before.

I became alarmed. Then one of the nurses told me that there was a visiting doctor waiting to talk with me. He was a young man and a foreigner who introduced himself as Dr. Mahfouz. He wasn't white. In fact he was darker than your father, but in that hospital he was considered white because he was from another country. I liked him right away.

He said he wanted to try something new, a new kind of skin grafting. What he wanted to do, with my permission, was take some of my skin from my outer thigh between the knee and the hip and graft it onto your face. I quickly said, Yes. He then said, After I finish, you will have to stay overnight in the hospital. Your thigh will heal quickly. That night, I told your father, and he said, Do what you have to do. He didn't

85

seem all that interested. He was like most men of his generation. The care of infants and children was women's work.

The next day, a Wednesday, the operation was performed. With a fresh bandage on my thigh, I left the hospital the following day, but you had to stay. The scar remained with me and in time came to look like a birthmark. Friday and Saturday, I visited you during visiting hours. And it was good to see that you were recovering nicely.

Although it was raining on Sunday, I wanted to go to the hospital to see you, but Clarence wasn't anywhere in sight and I had no way of contacting him. Lately, once again, we hadn't been getting along well. There was no point in waiting around for him. And I'd missed the bus. So I walked the three miles all the way to the hospital. And by the time I got there, soaking wet, visiting hours were almost over.

Just as I was climbing the steps, Clarence and his new friend Leroy Park—called Brother Leroy—and Brother Leroy's daughter, Savina, who was about my age, were coming down the steps. We passed with a great deal of uneasiness. I was soaking wet, dripping, literally, and here was Clarence, ironically, able and willing to drive his friends to the hospital to see his son, but not his wife. I was hurt.

Soon after I brought you home, I got pregnant again. But I didn't know it right away. Meanwhile, I hadn't gone back to work yet. I was home taking care of you.

The nurse had told me how to wash the area operated on, and it was easy. It helped that you were not a fussy baby, especially because I was learning as I went along.

It was around this time that Clarence sent for his older brother, Alvin, in Chicago. He wanted Alvin to help him run a new restaurant he'd just opened over on the coast in Savannah. Clarence ran a gambling business upstairs over the restaurant. Alvin was a top-notch cook, and Clarence wanted his brother to do the cooking even though he knew his brother was an alcoholic.

Now that I was pregnant again, my sisters and neighbors came over and helped me as much as possible. Once in a while I'd go over to Carrie's to visit, but even with my friends and relatives around, it was a lonesome life. I was suffering with depression, too. Had I known marriage was going to be like this, I would not have let myself be lulled into it. Pregnant again, I felt even more trapped—by marriage, by my own body, by my inability to see a way out.

Also, Clarence's two new businesses—the upstairs one and the downstairs one—weren't doing extremely well. Savannah welcomed his businesses! Customers and players were not the problem. The problem was his own gambling sickness. As fast as Alvin and the waitresses took in money, Clarence would come down and take it upstairs and gamble it away. He was like a burning fuse. And I prayed there would not be an explosion.

Christmastime. You were now a year old. Clarence spent quite a bit of money making a nice Christmas for us that year. He bought a big Christmas tree and an electric train and a red fire chief car and other presents for you. And he bought me presents, too. My sisters also brought presents for you. Clarence paid the rent and filled the icebox and the kitchen shelves with groceries.

A day or two after Christmas, I dressed you up and Clarence took you out to show you off to his friends, took you to the barbershop down on The Corner. That was what they called Five Points, which was the Negro business district. It was where five streets came together. All of Clarence's friends and flunkies sang his praise for having such a fine-looking little boy. When the two of you returned, my heart was heavy. I didn't trust this happiness. The fuse was still burning. That night Clarence left to go back to Savannah.

And soon he lost both the restaurant and the gambling business. When that happened he and Alvin together came back to Atlanta. Clarence was mean as a snake. His eyes were narrow and red with anger. I was scared to say anything, even How are you?, to him. This was late January, about two weeks before I was due to go into the hospital to have my second child.

Then came the time when I had to speak. When I asked Clarence to please pay the grocery bill, he grabbed my hair and slammed the top of my head into the wall repeatedly. This was the first time he'd ever hit me.

I was facing him and I could see his teeth gritting. He hurt me bad. I'd never been hit like that by anybody. This was drastic. Then he stomped out of the house. I was left on the floor in tears and terrified.

Lying there, I wondered what had set him off. I didn't then realize how humiliated he felt by his own self-defeat. I also didn't know how the loss of self-esteem could make a man so violent. I couldn't get beyond his dislike for me. It hurt me deeply.

The storekeeper wouldn't sell us any more food till the bill was paid. Was that asking too much? It was not, from my point of view. But it was, from Clarence's. My asking him for money he didn't have hurt his pride. I had forgotten about his pride. What good was pride in the face of hunger? I remembered my brothers and Pa. My sisters and I never had the problem of pride. We were proud women, but we were not like the men. And it never occurred to me that Clarence might not have enough money to pay the grocery bill. Despite his hurt pride, there was no excuse for what he did to me.

Alvin came by later that same day and told me the whole story of how Clarence lost everything by gambling and how badly he had treated him in Savannah. Alvin said he was going to go back to Chicago, but that he needed to work somewhere for a while here in Atlanta till he made himself enough money to pay his way. I felt sorry for him.

➤

Two days later, a neighbor came to take you out for a ride in the stroller. And while I was putting warm clothes on you, I suddenly felt a little pain in the stomach area.

There was a telephone in a store, near Clarence's new business place on Currier Street, where I could call him if I needed to. The problem was, I was scared to call, scared to ask him to do anything for me—even scared to ask him to take me to the hospital.

But the pains kept on coming. So I braced myself and called Clarence, anyway. He came rushing home in a borrowed car and drove me to Grady. He waited in the waiting room while I was with the doctor. The doctor said my pain was gas and gave me a small block of magnesium. When I returned to the waiting room and told Clarence, he gritted his teeth. Fear leaped around my heart.

Although he didn't say anything on the way back, I knew by his expression and silence that he was mad as an upset pit bull. His eyes flashed and he kept clinching his teeth. And he was driving fast—starting and stopping fast and making the tires squeak. Then what I expected happened. He hit me with his fist upside my head. And I could do nothing but sit there with tears running down my cheeks. The pain moved through my head in large electric waves.

Seven

When labor did actually start, I went to Grady in an ambulance. My memory of the birth of your sister Serena Mae wasn't clear the way the first birth was. But I remembered in the hospital my two sisters coming to see me. They had been so good to me during my pregnancy, and I was grateful.

I also remembered coming home from the hospital. Miss Anna came and stayed with me the first two days. But Mama didn't come to be with me this time. Both my sisters though were there to help, as usual, helping with you, with diapers and feeding, and with whatever else they could do. The doctor wanted me to come back in six weeks.

By now I had started making dresses for other women just to have some kind of dependable income for the house and you children. It was one of the great skills Mama taught me, one that sustained me through hard times. Three of my close-by neighbors, Annie, Birdie and Cristina, were my first customers. I loved listening to the stories and neighborhood gossip they told me.

Two decades later. For a while I was a self-employed seamstress working at home in Chicago, and once again enjoying the stories my customers told me. Three of the most interesting were Lulu, Ned and the dead woman.

A high-class prostitute, Lulu lived in an apartment on the other side of the court. At first I knew her only in passing, like I knew so many other neighbors. Then one day she called for an appointment.

She then brought six dresses she had bought from the Pint Size Shop in the Loop. She wanted them adjusted right away. And she sat and talked with me while I worked on the dresses. When I finished them Lulu tipped me fifty dollars, and thereafter she became one of my best customers.

On that first visit Lulu said, I spent last night at the Lake Michigan Plaza Hotel with a well-known politician who wants me to go to Washington with him. But Lulu said she wasn't even considering it. The politician was white and the black bellhops had to sneak her in to see him by way of the freight elevator. This was common practice for her.

Lulu knew most of the bellhops in the big hotels in the Loop. Negroes were still not welcome in most hotels downtown. So she couldn't walk in the front door and through the lobby like white prostitutes did without attracting attention. Lulu worked only the Loop and white men. But the bellhops were risking their jobs sneaking her in and out through the back way.

On the day after Christmas, Lulu came over and told me she'd spent Christmas Day in jail. The story went this way. It was three in the morning when a security man at the Grand Hotel Wabash, in the Loop, caught sight of her coming out of a room on the eleventh floor. She ran—took off her heels and ran so fast he couldn't catch her. She said, Honey, all he saw was a black streak pass in front of him.

She ran all the way down the stairway to the first floor and into the lobby. At one point in her running, she ran into the lounge—the Cool Breeze Bar—trying to duck him. No one was there. She jumped behind the bar. She knocked over a display of liquor bottles—Old Crow, White Horse, Old Grand Dad, Jim Beam, the rest of them all fell over like bowling pins.

Lulu said she turned over chairs and tables and threw them behind her, trying to trip the security man. Or at least slow him down. But she got tired and he caught her, finally, in the back near the freight elevator.

For two years she'd worked the Loop and never before been caught. Turning tricks was getting to be too hard. Now Lulu said she was going to marry a plain working man who'd been after her to tie the knot with him for a long time. His name was Ajax Byrd. But she was going to keep working for the time being. She said, Ajax doesn't make the kind of money I need to maintain myself, Inez.

Ned was a big man who weighed about two hundred and fifty pounds. He sat on the couch and explained, in great detail, just what he wanted for this upcoming holiday season—one white-sequinned dress and one black one. For each dress, Ned wanted a small waistline and a huge bosom. And he wanted me to get everything for him.

I told him that I could do the work. But I looked all over Chicago before I found high heels large enough for his big feet. Then I went to a corset shop with my tape measure and measured corsets before choosing the right two. At home, I padded the bra cups till they were giant-size, and altered the waistline till Cinderella could have worn the thing. I worked on the sequins and adjusted them to the corsets. When Ned came over for a fitting, the whole getup was so tight I had to help him into it. But once he was in, he loved it.

Ned thereafter became a regular customer for the next four years. When he was dressed up in his female outfit he insisted people call him Lady Nedda, but I never called him anything but Ned. When he moved his beauty shop farther south, I lost him as a customer.

The dead woman was very much alive when she came to me. She was an expert on preschool education and lectured on the subject all over the country. She became a regular customer. On this particular day she came to pick up an outfit I'd made for her to wear to Nashville, where she had a speaking engagement.

She left my place around two in the afternoon, and

later that night, just after I'd turned off the light at eleven and was about to fall asleep, the phone rang. A man told me that my customer was dead. He was calling people listed in her address book. He said she died on the train just before it pulled out of Polk Street Station.

I'd just seen her and talked with her and now she was dead. There was something unsettling about having a human being alive one moment, breathing and talking with you, then suddenly dead—even one not close to you. It cut us all down to size.

A couple of days later, I went to the funeral parlor, before they put her body on display, to make sure the new dress was fitting properly. Just as I suspected, with her lying down it was too short on her—and undignified—in the casket, although it had fit her fine standing.

So I told the director that I wanted to take the dress back home and make a few alterations. And I am sure this was a very unusual request. He just looked at me, then nodded. I waited in his office for the dress, and ten minutes later he brought it out in a brown paper bag.

I took it home and sewed a flounce onto it so that it would cover her knees—a pretty ornamental flounce with lots of pinks and light greens. In death—maybe especially in death—a person needed dignity. It was the least I could do. The fact that the alteration had not been requested was of no concern to me. I felt better.

My customer's funeral was at Roberts' Temple. Five preachers were in the pulpit. Hundreds of people packed the church. The Chicago Defender *said she was only forty-one. Although she was a customer and not a close friend, I liked and admired her. And her death left a sadness in me that I couldn't shake for a long time.*

But even as I made dresses and brought in money, Clarence's mistreatment continued. When he hit me in the face and broke a front tooth, once again I packed two suitcases and took you children and left the house. I was broke. I couldn't turn to my sisters for money. They'd already given me all they could. A neighbor of ours, Mr. Walker, had a taxi service. So I got him to drive me to Carrie's, where I left you and my suitcases.

Then Mr. Walker drove me to Peachtree Street to see Mr. Silverstone, the white man Mama took care of when he was an infant. That was before she moved back to Dublinville from Atlanta and got married. I showed Mr. Silverstone the Christmas card envelope Mama had given me for such an occasion, and it had his return address on it. I watched his face as he examined his own envelope.

I told him that I was Ada's youngest daughter, and that I needed bus fare to go home. He looked at me carefully. What was he thinking? There seemed to be a question at the tip of his tongue, but he finally decided against giving voice to it. I was trying not to cry, but I felt awful having to beg for money. This was something I'd never done before.

Mr. Silverstone gave me some money, and I thanked him. Then Mr. Walker, who'd waited in his taxi, drove me back to Carrie's. I picked up you children and the suitcases. By the time I got to the station the bus I meant to catch to Dublinville was already pulling out of the station.

I had to wait a long time for the next one. It would be the late bus, and the last to leave the station that night. So I sat there on the hard wooden bench with you for hours. Off and on, Serena slept on my lap, and you played on the bench next to me till you were bored and fell asleep, too.

By the time I got to the filling station in Dublinville, where the bus stopped, it was ten o'clock at night. So I asked the driver—a white man, of course—if he would let me out at the Hull place right over the hill. Drivers always did that for people, even colored people.

But this one said no. He had those mean narrow eyes you saw so often in the faces of poor and angry white men. I had the feeling that for some reason he'd taken a personal dislike for me. Why was beyond me. I didn't even want to try to imagine.

Fumbling and stumbling, I got out with you children and my two suitcases and stood there on the sidewalk. I looked around. There were no lights on anywhere, and all the stores were closed. Not a person in sight. I couldn't find the words for how heartbroken I felt that night, standing shivering in the darkness, with crickets burping in the stillness. It was impossible to walk to Mama's with children and suitcases.

Without much hope, I stood there waiting for, and hoping for, somebody to come along. Serena was asleep on my shoulder. You were sitting on one of the suitcases. Then I saw headlights slowly approaching. Good, I thought, it's probably the sheriff. He'd give me a lift. And the car stopped right in front of me. I couldn't see at first who was inside, but it was not the sheriff's car. I saw two white men in the front, and nobody in back.

I looked closer. They were two of Corrie Webster's three sons—Melvin, the oldest, and Russell, the youngest. Melvin was in the driver's seat, and he got out, then Russell got out. Russell was taller than his older brother, and better looking, with darker hair and gentle eyes. But the middle boy, Owens, was better looking than both Melvin and Russell. Melvin had his daddy's eyes—eyes of distant sorrow.

We exchanged greetings. They asked what had happened. I told them about the bus driver refusing my request. Melvin and Russell picked up my suitcases and put them in the trunk of the car. Russell then lifted you into the back seat. Melvin held the baby while I got myself in next to you, then Melvin handed the baby in to me. The car smelled like cigarette smoke.

I asked how they were doing—asked about their brother, Owens. They were fine, he was fine. I'd heard that Old Lady Daphne, their grandmother, had passed away in 1936. Melvin said he himself was in college in Athens, studying to be a lawyer, and that he was finding it hard going.

Russell laughed and said, If you don't keep them grades up, the old man ain't going to keep paying your tuition. But Russell didn't say anything about himself. Everybody knew he was turning out like his daddy. Although well dressed every day just like his father, he'd started drinking and hanging around the gas station like a ne'er-do-well.

I thought of their father, and almost asked about him, but I knew better. Had I had the nerve to do so, the question might have opened a can of worms too wiggly for them to handle. I myself might not have been able to handle the consequences, either. I could imagine a conversation between the three of us derailing into embarrassment, accusations and recriminations.

Instead, I said, I hope your folks are well. They're fine, they said. I felt a little tension between us at that moment. Maybe it was my imagination, but I didn't think so. I think the tension was stemming from what we were *not* saying to each other, what we could never say, dared not say—though we could not stop thinking about it.

They didn't say much after that—just how are you, and that sort of thing. They'd heard that I'd moved to Atlanta and was married. I guess there wasn't much else to say with ease. I said I was all right. I didn't want to go into detail. I felt that my life would have been of no interest to them.

What could I have said? My husband mistreats me? I'm brokenhearted? I feel trapped in an awful marriage? I couldn't talk about my life to strangers. And it was all too painful to talk about it to people I knew—and my blood white brothers, I knew the least of all. But I sure was grateful for the ride.

They drove me to Mama's and pulled into the driveway and parked by the walkway. I saw, through the window, a light come on in the house. Mama was getting up. A moment later she came to the door and said, Who's there? And I called back, It's me, Inez. Then she came out onto the porch in her robe.

Russell lifted you out of the back seat, and carried you up and stood you on the front porch, then returned. I could hear Mama talking to you, but you weren't answering. You were tired and sleepy.

Russell and Melvin carried my suitcases all the way inside the front door. I followed, carrying the baby, and I thanked them, and Mama thanked them. They said, You're welcome. And Mama said, God sure enough sent you boys to help this girl. And they nodded and said, Glad we could help. Good night, Miss Hull, good night, Inez.

I wasn't there long before Clarence and Miss Anna came one afternoon. And Mama told him off but good. Miss Anna, being a sanctified preacher, just sat there biting her fingernails. Then she wanted to pray for us, but Mama told her to pray for herself. So she just sat there looking like her feelings were hurt.

Then Clarence got up and walked out to the car and came back with packages. He said they were toys and new clothes for you children. Mama called you. You were out in the yard on your knees playing in the dirt. You came up on the porch and took the red truck your father held out to you. There was a doll for Serena, but it was as big as she was. It was not the right thing for an infant. A rattle would have been better. Mama held the doll, trying to get Serena to touch its face.

Clarence then pressed a roll of money into my hand and said, This is for you. I looked at the money, and although I was still feeling very hurt, and very abused, I managed to whisper thank you to him, because I was taught to always be polite—even to a skunk. Plus, I needed the money. I was flat broke. And he had a right to support his children. After three or four hours, he and his mother said good-bye and drove off.

Time moved slowly here. And just before Christmas, Clarence came back again, but alone, bringing shoes and more new clothes for you children. Serena was walking good by now. Each morning I enjoyed the freshness of waking up in the country, in the house where I grew up, where everything was familiar. This house gave me a strong sense of who I was. I felt comfort here that I was unable to feel anywhere else.

Meanwhile, down the road, a neighbor girl, Vanessa Strong, about sixteen, had been dying to get out of Dublinville. Vanessa wanted to go to Atlanta and stay with me. In exchange for food and shelter, she said she would look after you kids and help me with

101

housework. If it was okay with me it was okay with her folks.

Clarence's oldest sister, Estelle—another "yellow" girl—was now operating one of the elevators at the Piedmont. She wrote to me and said that Mr. Paxton was expecting me back to work as soon as Serena was walking. I had the feeling that Clarence might have put her up to writing that letter.

But I was hesitating to go back to him. Although he was telling me he was a changed man, I didn't trust him. He had lied to me before. I felt foolish even thinking about going back. And I was thinking about it. I was trying to sell myself on the wisdom of going back.

Maybe with Vanessa in the house, things might be different. After all, there was part of me that still wanted my marriage to work. It seemed, at the time, that if the marriage failed all the way, I too was a failure—a complete failure. Looking back, I saw how silly that idea was, but that was how I felt at the time. But if I went back, I wanted Clarence to respect me, and be kind to me. Kindness was what I wanted most from him—the very thing he couldn't give anymore. I was hoping against hope.

Well, I did go back. No surprise there. And Vanessa went with me. And after I was back on my job for a while, I started to feel better about myself. But Clarence's habits hadn't changed. He spent almost no time with us.

At home I cooked and washed and ironed for my family and did some sewing to earn the money we needed. Sometimes Clarence gave me money for our upkeep, sometimes he didn't. Vanessa played with you children and washed the dishes.

Once Estelle came by on my day off. Clarence was home that day. Estelle had a boyfriend who was driving a truck for a carpet salesman who lived at the Piedmont, but the boyfriend was about to leave for a better-paying job, driving for Coca-Cola, like my brother Wilbur. The carpet man needed a new driver, and Estelle wanted to know if her brother wanted the job.

To my surprise, Clarence said yes. And he took the job. I almost let myself believe that this was a good sign, that he was about to straighten up—as they used to say—and fly right. I kept my fingers crossed and I prayed.

But Clarence kept that job only four days. His last trip was to Monroe to some store where he had to drop off carpets. It was heavy, hard work, and his hands were soft. He wasn't used to hard work. He quit the morning of the fifth day. He never again showed up for work.

While these things were happening, Vanessa was getting homesick. And I accepted the fact that she was going to leave soon. So I was making her some pretty dresses to take back home with her. Then, finally, Clarence and I drove Vanessa back to Dublinville one Saturday afternoon.

I went back to relying on a neighborhood girl, Bay Bay, to help me with the baby-sitting while I worked.

In the locker room at the Piedmont the white girls I worked with talked about where they went, and about their husbands and boyfriends. But I was quiet. I didn't have much to say in return. They all had working husbands or boyfriends. I didn't want them to know my situation. I was ashamed of it.

For a while, after Vanessa left, Clarence treated me pretty well, then the bad treatment started up again. He blackened my eye and broke my nose with his fist. When these things happened I made up my mind then that I was leaving him. My marriage and becoming a mother were the most important things in my life up till then. Now it looked like permanent separation and divorce were about to be added to that list. I just wanted to finish up a couple of dresses I was working on, and get them to my customers before leaving. I couldn't go on like this. This was it. I was sure this time.

Eight

After a doctor examined and x-rayed my nose he advised me against having the bone reset. It's not a bad break, he said. It'll heal on its own. And he was right. With the slightly irregular line of my nose, my face didn't look bad.

But I knew I couldn't go back to work with a messed-up face. They wouldn't allow me on the elevator with a black eye. So I called Estelle and told her to tell the boss that I couldn't come in. And although I told her why, she said she'd tell Mr. Paxton that one of the children was sick.

That Monday evening, around the time people were coming home from work, Clarence came home and without saying anything, started changing his clothes. I knew him well enough to know that he was mad about something. While changing pants he pulled his belt out and wrapped part of it around his hand, then came at me like a bull. He grabbed my arm, but I finally got free and ran out the front door.

An elderly woman across the street was on her front porch. She saw what was happening. Rushing right up to Clarence, she slammed him across his head as hard as she could with a bed slat. And she shouted in his face, Don't you ever hit this girl again! You hear me, you brute?

And he backed away from her and her slat. In fact, she drove him all the way to his car, in front of our house, and he jumped in and sped away, all the while looking back at her shaking her slat at him.

I knew this was the end. And each time I said this to myself, I believed it. But this time I wasn't in a hurry. I walked slowly back into the house and started packing, just the two small suitcases of our clothes. I was taking only a few things we needed.

After I got the things together that I would be taking with me, I went around to my neighbors' and over to Carrie's, to Saffrey's, to Brenna's and told them I would be leaving Atlanta. I told Minnie and Estelle, too. I had a little bit of money I'd saved from dressmaking.

That following Tuesday, the day I was supposed to go back to work, I got Mr. Walker to load my stuff in his taxi. He helped me get you children into the car. As we drove off, I waved good-bye to my neighbors as they watched from their windows. Tears were brimming in my eyes. But everybody knew I'd taken all I could and then some. So Mr. Walker drove us to the bus station and I paid him and said good-bye to him, too.

When I got home, Mama and Pa saw my condition, and said that leaving was the right thing to do. In fact, Pa went into town and talked with Sheriff Dusty Ogburn about my situation. When Pa came back he said the sheriff had agreed to drive me back to Atlanta. He would wait with me while I got the rest of my things.

The next morning Sheriff Ogburn picked me up around six and we hit the road. When we got into Atlanta he spotted a policeman and stopped and got out to talk with him. This was in front of Sears Roebuck downtown. When the sheriff returned, he told me that he himself had no authority in Atlanta, but that the policeman would come with us.

Sheriff Ogburn helped me while the policeman stood on the front porch. He said I could take only clothing. There was a beautiful spread on the bed that Mama had made for me. We piled our clothes into it and he tied it. After that, I got a sheet and we filled that up, too, and tied it. He put these bundles in the back of his car.

Everybody was on their porches watching me escorted by these two big white men. Returning to the sheriff's car, I felt hurt, embarrassed and angry.

As we drove off, once again I waved good-bye and they waved back. And the policeman said to Sheriff Ogburn, Anytime you need me to help protect a cute little gal like this against her nigger, you just let me know.

The policeman grinned at me, but I refused to look

at him. Then he said to me, If that nigger husband of yours bothers you again, you just call me. Okay?

And I still said nothing. Then he said, What's the matter, cat's got your tongue? Then I just looked at him and said, No sir.

I stayed at Mama's this time again for quite a long time. Clarence came every so often, but now never with Miss Anna. Clarence and I talked, and I was polite but cool toward him. He never said anything to me about coming back. It was as though he knew this was the end—without being told.

Eventually a letter came from Carrie and in the same envelope my old bodyguard and friend Blake had stuck in a note. Blake just said he was doing fine and he hoped that I was getting along okay. I hadn't seen much of Blake during my life with Clarence, although he was close to him. And in fact, at various times, Blake had worked for Clarence in Buttermilk Bottom, a place I never visited.

Carrie's letter said that Clarence was now swimming in money. She said he'd bought trucks, and had a trucking business on the side as a kind of cover for his shady dealings. He'd moved into another house, this one on Currier Place. Clarence and Brother Leroy were running a new gambling house together. They were also writing policy out of a filling station where they held half-ownership. And Clarence now owned a restaurant down on Fulton.

I disliked what I was thinking, disliked my own weakness, the trapped condition I felt myself to be in. It was a miserable feeling. I prayed for calmness in myself because only from a calm state could I begin to find my way.

With Carrie's letter on my lap, I remembered what Miss Bellamy, the nursery school and preschool teacher in Atlanta, had told me. Preschool children had to be toilet-trained before she'd take them. She'd promised to help me by admitting you and Serena as soon as you were toilet-trained or old enough.

Once again, I was about to act against my own better judgment. But I felt like I was making no progress in Dublinville. Going to church on Sunday, helping Mama, and taking care of children was my whole life at the time. A calmness I liked was coming over me. I felt stagnant, like I was going nowhere fast. But I also knew that in going back I was no longer willing to endure the abuse.

My oldest sister Lowella came home from Chicago for a visit. It was good to see her. She was more self-assured, a city woman. She told me she was worried about how quiet I had become. Lowella said, You're not yourself. You've always been a very talkative person. She said she wished I'd come to Chicago and visit her. Just for a change of pace. She thought it would lift my spirit.

I kept the thought of Chicago in my mind as I packed once again, and moved us back to Atlanta. Clarence welcomed me back, and I moved into his new Currier Place house. This was the third time I'd moved into a fully furnished place he provided. Friends of his had arranged the house. When I got there, I wanted a few changes, so I went ahead and made them. That was okay by Clarence.

Right away I took you to Miss Bellamy's to enroll you. But Serena hollered and cried so much, because she didn't want to leave her brother, that Miss Bellamy said, Just leave her, too. You weren't happy either about being left there without your sister. I'll take both of them, said Miss Bellamy. And she did.

Aunt Irene was Edith Jackson's daughter, grown up now. She was the infant Rebecca said should not nurse at the same breast her own baby Anna was to nurse at. I called Irene Aunt although she wasn't a blood relative. She'd come from Chicago for a funeral in Hutchinson. She'd moved to Chicago some years before. After the funeral, she stopped in Dublinville to visit her adopted sister, Anna. They hadn't seen each other for some years. Then she stopped in Atlanta to visit other relatives and friends. I met Aunt Irene at the bus station.

I took her to my house and cooked dinner for her. Although in a way she was Clarence's aunt, he didn't take much interest in her. She stayed one night with us. Before leaving the next afternoon she said, Inez, you ought to come visit me in Chicago sometime. This was my second Chicago invitation. And I said, I just might do that, Aunt Irene.

When she got back to Chicago, she wrote to me and thanked me for my hospitality. And I kept in touch with her. You and Serena, meanwhile, were doing fine in preschool but home life wasn't so hot. Clarence had women pulling after him left and right. Everybody all over town knew about him and his women. He didn't even try to hide it from me. I still had feelings for him even after all the abuse, but a kind of numbness had also lodged itself in me. Clarence was a habit, a bad habit.

One night a cousin of mine, Enid Douglas, called me. She, too, was visiting from Chicago. I invited her over and made dinner for her. Clarence happened to come in while she and I were eating dinner. She said, Clarence, I want you to send Inez to visit me in Chicago. He smiled. He said, Sure. And she said, Clarence, I'm serious now. Don't be kidding me. And he said, I'm serious, too. Any time Inez wants to go, she can go. She knows that.

So this was the third person who'd made Chicago seem possible. After that, I made up my mind to visit Chicago. Meanwhile Clarence had bought nice clothes for you children and me and I had started feeling like I was somebody. I was going to a few places, but very seldom anyplace with him.

I once wanted to go to a club on Auburn Avenue to a dance. I told Clarence I had two tickets. I showed them to him. And he promised he'd go with me, but when the time came he changed his mind and got

111

Blake to take me. So, Blake dressed up and drove me to the dance in Clarence's new Cadillac.

And Clarence drove off somewhere in his truck. At the dance there were people I knew—neighbors of Carrie's, friends from the old neighborhoods, even a couple of people I'd known since I was nine at David T. Howard. Blake and I got a table, ordered drinks, danced a couple of times, and stopped at various tables to chat. The dance floor was polished wood. I did the Black Bottom and the Camel Walk with Blake and a few others. And I felt light and carefree for the first time in years. I was surprised at my ability to still feel lighthearted, to laugh, to socialize, to dance. I hadn't danced since my roommate Laura and I used to practice dancing when our landlady wasn't around.

I didn't witness this. I learned about it later. A few weeks after the dance, Clarence and a woman friend of his were in his car near Spelman College on the other side of town. They pulled out from the curb into traffic and just at that point, a little girl ran out from between two cars, smack into the side of Clarence's car. He couldn't react or stop fast enough. He ran over her. When this happened, the woman got out and walked away, I guess so she wouldn't be involved when the police came. But people on the sidewalk saw her leave. There were witnesses—unfortunately for Clarence.

He jumped out of the car. He was very upset. He

picked up the child and rushed her to Grady. The girl's father followed in his own car. When Clarence got home, he said he wanted me to say I was the woman with him in his car. He'd already put my name on the police report that he had to fill out at the hospital. On the report he said that I left the car to go home to see about my children.

Although I said no, because I wasn't going to lie for him, I did go to see the girl's parents. And I took them some money Clarence gave me to give them. But after two weeks the child died.

The police came to the house to talk to me because the report said I was in the car. I didn't know anything about it, and told them I didn't. I said it wasn't me. I wasn't going to lie for him, no matter what he did to me. Naturally, Clarence was mad about my not lying for him, but this time his anger didn't cause him to hit me.

He then started giving the dead girl's parents money every week. Not that they'd asked for it. It was something Clarence felt he needed to do. He'd paid for the funeral and the burial, too. The father had been home baby-sitting when it happened.

One time I stopped by there, to drop off the money, and the mother said, Inez, I don't blame your husband. I blame my own husband. Our daughter would be alive today if he'd been watching her like he was supposed to do. She said she appreciated the money, but that she didn't blame Clarence.

Then, at a certain point, she told me to tell Clarence

113

not to send her any more money. Money won't bring my daughter back, she said. Tell him he doesn't have to feel guilty about it. But when I repeated her words to Clarence he said, Just keep taking them the money. They'll take it. Meanwhile, he was having nightmares about the little girl, even when he tried to sleep in the daytime. He was in bad shape.

When I wouldn't take the money anymore, Clarence himself drove over there and tried to make them take it. But as a result, he got himself into the middle of a big family argument. The mother and father now weren't getting along so well, since their daughter's death.

Clarence's reaction to the death of the little girl gave me a view of a side of him I didn't know existed. He showed a capacity for guilt and he felt compassion for the girl's parents. Naturally I couldn't help wondering why he was incapable of feeling compassion for, or even just kindness toward, me.

And this day they were in the middle of a shouting match. Then when they noticed Clarence standing there in their living room, trying to give them money, both of them turned on him, and pushed him out of the house, and told him to stay out of their business. We don't want your money, she shouted. So he never went back.

One day when Blake drove you children home from Miss Bellamy's, he handed me a note from her. I read it and saw that she wanted me to come to school as soon as possible. Blake had walked on back to the kitchen to get a drink of water.

So the next day when Blake was driving to Miss Bellamy's, I rode in the truck with him. Miss Bellamy wanted to show me something. She had drawings children had made pinned up on the wall. I looked at the drawings and they all looked very nice.

Miss Bellamy asked if I saw anything different about the car in your drawing. I couldn't see anything different. Then she said, Clarence's car has four wheels. All the other cars have only two. She said that this was a sign of exceptional ability, and that I should always encourage you, and one day you would make me proud. I never forgot that, and I always did encourage you to be original and to think for yourself.

A rumor was going around the neighborhood. Clarence's restaurant was about to go out of business. I didn't know much about the restaurant. I had been in there only a few times. Clarence sometimes took you and Serena there for ice cream and cake. You loved sitting on the swivel stools at the counter because you could turn around and around. But I knew one thing: If Clarence lost the restaurant, he would be difficult to get along with.

During this time, I probably saw more of Blake than I did of Clarence, because Blake was there in the morning to take you children to school, and he brought you home in the afternoon. He was somebody

I could talk with. It helped that I had known him since I was eight. He'd always been good to me.

One time Blake told me that in his opinion Clarence had never loved me. He said, All Clarence ever wanted you for was to show you off, to show the world that he has a beautiful wife. You're just a trophy to Clarence. And Blake said, But he don't like your proud spirit. He's been trying to break your spirit from day one. Can't you see that?

Blake also said that Clarence, who'd grown up in the streets, didn't care for people who'd been brought up sheltered like I was. He dislikes them a lot, Blake said. It's really jealousy. What Blake was saying made sense.

Then Blake went on to say that he'd taken care of me when I was a little girl but that now that I was grown, I had better start taking care of myself. Blake said, He don't love you. Never have! It's time you woke up. When you go to see your people in Chicago, you stay there. You're wasting your time with this man.

I thought about what Blake had said. I *was* proud and Clarence had almost destroyed my pride. And although I never thought of myself as beautiful, I understood what Blake was talking about. I didn't doubt that Clarence, in some twisted way, thought of me as something to show off, a *thing*.

I thought seriously about staying in Chicago. But he perhaps resented the fact that I was also a person with opinions, feelings and needs. There was a lot of truth in what Blake said, but there were things about Clarence that I knew more about than Blake ever could. Clarence, for one thing, had a low tolerance for intimacy, mentally, emotionally and physically. He didn't trust anybody, not even me, or especially not me. He needed desperately to control all his encounters with people. Many years later it became clear to me that he was so fragile inside that the iron wall he'd constructed around himself was designed to protect that fragility that was essentially Clarence. So possessing me was part of maintaining and controlling the world around him.

for the war in Europe. All my neighbors meanwhile

Nine

The army called Clarence downtown for a physical, but when they saw how flat-footed he was, he was rejected. Eight months earlier—back in January 1942—boys in our neighborhood had started leaving for the war in Europe. All my neighbors meanwhile kept shaking their heads and saying how much worse things were going to get before they'd get better.

You would be six at the end of the year and Serena would be five in February. I was making plans to visit Chicago, so I told Miss Bellamy you children wouldn't be there for a month. I paid her for that month anyway. That was her rule. Then Clarence and I drove you and Serena down to Mama's that weekend. I couldn't let myself be stopped by the guilt I felt for leaving. I knew you were in good hands with Mama. Back in Atlanta, I went shopping for a few things for myself and left for Chicago two days later.

The train ride to Chicago was quite an adventure. I'd never been on such a long journey alone before. It felt strange and wonderful. Of course I was in the rundown colored car, but once we crossed the Mason–Dixon line, colored people got up and moved to better seats farther up in the train. The lady next to me looked at me and said, You going to stay here? I said, Yes. She said, Girl, you better get yourself up and come on with me. This car smells like somebody's wet diaper.

In Chicago I stayed with my cousin, Enid Douglas, in her big rambling apartment on South Parkway (a street later renamed Martin Luther King Drive) in the 5800 block. She'd met me at the Polk Street Station. On the way to her place in a taxi, I was dazzled right away by the night lights, the wide boulevards, the many cars and the busyness of the city. And in the morning when I woke up, I looked out on the widest street I'd ever seen, one with three lanes, and two tree-lined parkways. Well-dressed Negroes were everywhere I looked, nobody in overalls. There were more people driving cars than walking.

Enid had cute dimples and she smiled a lot. She had just finished beauty school and she was working to save money to open her own shop. For the time being she was managing a chili joint called the Nickel Spot on Forty-seventh near South Parkway.

As soon as I was settled, I went to see Aunt Irene. She gave me a big hug. She hadn't aged a day. Still the same big woman with that round, freckled face, so open and friendly. Pretty soon after I got into town, she bought me a nice autograph book. And as I went along, I had my relatives and new friends write something in it by which I could remember my trip.

For one whole month I was going nonstop, visiting my sister Lowella and all my other relatives who had by then migrated to Chicago. In the daytime they took me to all kinds of places, such as the Field Museum and the Art Institute. At the Art Institute I thought of you and how much you liked to draw. You would love this place and would someday come to this place and see the great works of art.

At night we went to nightclubs on the South Side—the Club DeLisa's, Joe's, and the 411 Club. We saw the Nicholas Brothers, Screaming J Hawkins, Peg Leg Bates, Pearl Bailey, and others. The sparkling night lights were exciting. We ate at least twice at a popular place called Margie's Eat Shop. The aroma of spicy food was friendly. I saw Louis Jordan at the Capitol Lounge, saw a dance revue at the Regal Theater on Forty-seventh and South Parkway. Doing all this nightlife, I felt for the first time like a young woman. And I liked the sense of freedom I was beginning to feel.

My cousin Attorney Jesse Hull took me to my first Christian Science church service. I'd never seen such an orderly service. No shouting and jumping about. Not that I didn't sometimes enjoy Mama's type of church. But this was my kind of church. It was the kind of church I'd only heard about. The quiet dignity of the service appealed to me.

I had the feeling Aunt Irene and Attorney Jesse and my other relatives really cared about me, but they were also showing off their pretty relative from down home. That was fine by me. The more they thought I was pretty, the prettier I felt. I hadn't felt pretty since before I married.

I also went along with Cousin Jesse to two different courtroom trials and listened to him defend his clients. One case involved a man who'd lent his car to his cousin and the cousin wrecked it. The man was trying to make the cousin pay for his loss. The other was a case where a woman was before the judge to try to get more child support from her unemployed husband. The judge told the husband he'd better find a job or he was going to send him to jail.

I was truly impressed by Chicago, and as I was leaving, Aunt Irene told me that if I ever came back to live there, I could stay with her and her family till I got on my feet. And I thanked her and kept her offer in the back of my mind. No doubt about it, Chicago was a world I could move into on a moment's notice. I liked the new sense of myself it'd given me in just that brief time. Compared to Dublinville, Atlanta was a city. But Chicago was a city and a half compared to

Atlanta. And I wasn't about to forget the experience. I left the evening of October tenth.

On the train back to Atlanta, as I said at the beginning, I rode into the city as a white woman. I'd known for a long time that strangers often took me to be white unless I was in a setting where it suggested otherwise. So that was not new. That the conductor assumed I was white was not surprising. But the fact that he did make this assumption gave me a new sense of possibility. It was my first conscious taste of white privilege.

Conscious, because I could well have gotten up and moved to the smelly colored car on my own, but I chose not to. I stayed in the white car, not because I wanted to play white but because I made a deal with myself while sitting there. I said to myself, This proves, at least to me, that whiteness—or blackness, for that matter —is as thin as a ripple on the water.

I looked around and thought about the funny fact that despite the "one-drop law," I was lighter than half the people in that white car that morning. It made me wonder, What is this thing called whiteness? It certainly couldn't have much to do with the way a person looked, or with skin color, or with one's ancestors. It had to be mainly about the community a person was born into, and what that person was brought up believing.

Back at home, everybody said how well I looked. I'd gained ten pounds. I talked nonstop about Chicago and what I did. I now felt that I had the confidence to put some miles between Clarence and myself if things didn't get better.

The day after my return, Clarence and I drove to Dublinville to pick up you and Serena. It was good to see you, and you were happy to have me back. While I was in the kitchen helping Mama cook dinner that first night, I told her all about our relatives in Chicago. I also told her that if I ever left Clarence again I would not come to her, that I would be going to Chicago. Mama looked at me with her serious dark eyes and she nodded. That might work out better, she said. Mama was a woman of few words, but when she spoke you knew she meant what she said.

We got back to Atlanta, and back into our usual routine. Blake came Monday and took you children to Miss Bellamy's. My neighbors had plenty of gossip for me about what had happened on Currier Place while I was gone, and I listened to it all.

Brother Leroy's wife, Perfecta, came to see me and talked about what was going on in Clarence's and her husband's gambling house on Inman Street. She said Brother Leroy was thinking about pulling out from Clarence because of disagreements over money. I said, Perfecta, he never talks with me about his business. She said, You should make him tell you things. Leroy knows he'd better tell me. I thought, I can't imagine making Clarence do anything. Besides, by now I felt the less I knew about his business the better. I needed to focus on my children's and my own future.

Clarence knew I was not happy. He'd known it for a long time. The difference now was clear. He wanted to be free of me. One day he said, If you are so unhappy with me, maybe you ought to go back to Chicago where you can be happy. I said, Yes, that is exactly what I want to do. Good, then go, he said. So it was agreed.

We gathered your's and Serena's clothes and toys, paid Miss Bellamy the final bill, and drove you both to Mama's in Dublinville. I didn't let myself stop to think about my children missing me. If I had I would have torn up the ticket and stayed. I kept my mind focused on a future away from Clarence. And I knew that in a short time I would have you with me in Chicago.

By now you were so accustomed to going to and staying with Mama that it was already like a second home. But you had no way of knowing this time that I would be gone as long as I was. Before Clarence got in the car to drive back to Atlanta, he suggested that I stay a few days to help Mama get you children settled in.

Mama was already taking care of Lowella's two sons, Harry and Phillip, who were twelve and ten. Lowella was sending Mama a monthly check from Chicago to help pay their expenses. They were big for their ages. Harry was skinny and tall, and Phillip was short and stocky. They were big enough to help Mama in and around the house with chores. They worked the garden, fed the chickens and hogs, and brought in wood that Bert cut for the stove. The minute we got there you ran off to play with your cousins. And Serena stuck close to Mama in the kitchen, where the smell of baking cookies was very attractive.

After Clarence left, Mama said nonsense to his suggestion that I stay a few days. She said, That is just another one of his tricks. You go on and leave on the first bus in the morning. I said, All right. And early the next morning my brother Bert was there ready to drive me to the station. I'd decided that a long, tearful good-bye might upset you and Serena, so I kissed you in your beds while you slept and left quickly. It was still dark outside. Later, I wondered if staying a few days would have made any difference.

Bert dropped me off at the bus stop. My trip would have to wait, and I took the early bus back to Atlanta. A colored taxi drove me home. The house was empty. I got my clothes and packed them. I called a taxi and waited on the front porch.

Then I noticed a note on the kitchen table. My sister Brenna was at Grady having her first child. So that afternoon, I took the bus there to see her and the baby. Brenna was filled with joy over her baby. It was good to see her so happy.

I finally told her I was leaving for Chicago for good.

I could see she didn't believe me. No reason why she should. She knew how many times I'd left Clarence and returned. I hugged my sister and kissed her good-bye. That night I called Saffrey and told her my plans. I agreed to meet her for breakfast the next morning on my way to the train station.

I spent my last night with Clarence. He didn't touch me and I didn't touch him. That next morning I didn't kiss him good-bye or anything like that. I just looked in his eyes and thanked him again for the ticket. I then called a taxi and waited on the front porch till it came.

When it got there, the taxi driver helped me with my luggage. Clarence stood in the doorway watching and smiling. He didn't believe I was going for good, either. His expression told me that. But this time I knew. I knew things about myself now that he couldn't have known anything about.

I met Saffrey. She and I ate breakfast in a little cafe owned by a girlfriend of hers on Angier Avenue. We had eggs and sausage and grits. Then we walked out-side. It was not yet nine o'clock. You take care of your-self up there in Chicago—and come on back home, too, if things don't go well, she said. Saffrey didn't believe me, either. I kissed my sister good-bye, and got in one of the taxis sitting at the curb. In time, she would see. They all would see. I waved good-bye to Saffrey.

Once I was settled in my seat in the colored car and looking out the window, I thought about my life. I was moving north now. I would become myself, the full person I had not yet become. I would be myself, myself, myself, my whole woman self. But that would not change the way the world saw me. I knew the world would go on seeing me as either a black woman or a white woman.

And in some circumstances I would be either white or black. I knew it was likely. But that would not change the colorlessness inside me, would not change my effort to become fully myself, my quest for wholeness. That quest had more to do with myself as a woman dreaming of a better life. I was determined not to let race stand in my way, no matter how insistent it was. And I had no illusions. It was a huge stone placed in front of the cave of my humanity.

On the train, then and there, I also made up my mind that no man would ever again hit me. That was a promise to myself. Nobody would dog me ever again. And although I was angry about the damage Clarence had done to me, I also knew that something in me let him do it, and let it go on for so long. But I was past that weakness now and was stronger for having gotten through it.

And when finally the train pulled out of the station, I gazed a long while out the window at the houses and trees and telephone poles rushing by. In the distance a truck was moving along a road still wet from rain that came in the night. I watched till the sky turned dark blue. Then I closed my eyes and rested my head against the back of the seat.

When I got into Chicago, I called Aunt Irene from Polk Street Station. She sounded happy to hear my voice and said, Come on out, Nez. With my heart beating so loudly I could hear it above the roar of traffic, I took a taxi to her house on Garfield Boulevard.

Ten

I had brought with me less than $200, so I needed to go to work as soon as possible. I wanted to keep myself on a tight budget, too. Aunt Irene gave me a metal box and some little envelopes. I labeled them, "money to Mama for children," "food," "clothes," and so on. This would give me some structure. I then placed the envelopes in the box.

I was lucky. I soon went to work at the Nickel Spot, where Enid was still the manager. She told me I'd be mainly working the cash register. Her cook, Dion the Greek, told me not to eat before coming to work. I'll fatten you up, he said. I weighed about a 110 pounds at the time. Everybody said I was too skinny.

The two waitresses—DeEtte and Pam—who worked the morning shift were older than I was. I liked DeEtte and Pam, and I thought they liked me. DeEtte said, Watch out for Dion's pork chops. They'll give you heartburn. Pam said, And don't put too much trust in his french fries, either.

After a few weeks in Chicago, and on the job, I started feeling better about myself, although I thought all the time about my children. I felt guilty being away from them, yet this new feeling of self and freedom was a tonic. The pull kept me torn inside all the time. I dreamt about them and woke feeling guilty. Well, I kept telling myself, it's just a matter of time.

Aunt Irene wouldn't take any rent money from me, but I gave her husband eight dollars every week because they sent my sheets to the laundry with theirs. Plus, I used their phone. And on my day off, they made me feel welcome to food they cooked. I meanwhile sent the money I promised Mama every month. I'd promised myself that you children would be with me in one year—no longer. And I was working toward that goal.

I always bought the money orders at the nearby post office. One day a clerk told me I could start a savings account there. Aunt Irene agreed that it was a good idea. So I took $250 out of my metal box. I carried the cash to the post office and opened my new account.

I was trying my best to be careful with the money I was making. I tried to stretch every dollar. Aunt Irene and I soon stopped at a shop and put a coat I liked on layaway for me. Then I went to a department store and put some clothes on layaway to send you and Serena for Christmas. My plan was to pay off the layaway bills by the first day of December.

I went to Christian Science church every Sunday,

and I'd see my cousin Attorney Jesse Hull there. One Sunday I told Cousin Jesse that I was having a hard time dealing with guilt and fear—guilt about you children, and fear of the unknown future. He then made an appointment for me with a Christian Science practitioner, Isolde Meredith.

Miss Meredith lived on Forestville in the Forty-seventh block. She was a lovely woman with whom I could—and did—talk freely about my past. After I told her about myself, she advised me not to discuss my life with anyone else except God. She prayed with me and told me to feel free to call her whenever I needed to. After work, sometimes I'd stop to see Miss Meredith before I caught the jitney to go home. She helped me to control the guilt I felt for leaving you children.

Guilt and fear! I'd get over the guilt for a while after I'd talk with Miss Meredith, but then it would come right back. At times I was even afraid that I might run into Clarence on the street. Whenever a man showed any interest in me, I stopped him because I was scared he might turn out to be like Clarence. I didn't trust any man at this point.

One day when I got home, Aunt Irene had a letter from her sister saying that Clarence was coming to Chicago next month. I looked at the letter, recognizing Miss Anna's chicken-scratch penmanship. Clarence, according to his mother, wanted to stay at Aunt Irene's while visiting Chicago. That day at work I told Enid about his plan. She left the restaurant and ran across the street.

I could see her through the window over there talking on the sidewalk with a policeman. I recognized him as the officer who walked this end of Forty-seventh all the time. As Enid talked to him I watched her hands making quick gestures. And the officer kept nodding his head. Then Enid waved good-bye to him and came back across the street. In a low voice, so the customers couldn't hear, she said, Inez, I talked with Rabbit and he promised me he'd keep an eye on you. Okay?

Later, the officer stopped in and said, You're Inez. Right? Listen, he said, don't you worry. If you want me to, I can even stop your ex-husband from coming to Chicago. I said, How? He said, I'll show you. And he left and came back with three two-cent postcards and laid them on the counter. Write these cards to people you know will see him and don't put a return address on them.

So I wrote the cards to Miss Anna and Carrie and Blake. Rabbit took them and slid them in his shirt pocket. And I thanked him. Later he gave them to a lady friend of his who was a member of the Women's Auxiliary of the Brotherhood of Sleeping Car Porters.

She worked with the porters as a maid in the Pullman cars on the railroad between New York and Chicago. The next time she hit the road she took the cards with her, and she mailed them in New York City. And they arrived in Atlanta with a New York City postmark.

Aunt Irene didn't answer Miss Anna's letter. When

I saw Miss Meredith she said, Your Aunt Irene shouldn't be involved with this plan the policeman has worked out for you because Clarence is her kin. In fact, Miss Meredith suggested that I move. The idea of moving out of Aunt Irene's place didn't scare me as much as it might have a few months earlier.

Then Miss Meredith called a woman friend of hers named Sophie Bradford who said she would get me a place with the lady next door. But when I got to Sophie Bradford's flat, she took one look at me and said she wasn't going to send me next door. She said that she wanted me to stay with her instead. She said I looked like I could be her daughter and it was true. She was a light-complected older woman with a big smile, and I liked her right away.

After five and half months at Aunt Irene's, I moved into Sophie Bradford's ten-room flat with her and her husband, Jeremy. Right away, Sophie Bradford insisted that I call her Mama. And before long I was calling her just that and calling her husband Pops.

They both were from the South and it was easy for me to adjust to calling them by such intimate names. Extending the family beyond blood relatives was something we did all the time down South. When someone who was not a relative became close, we adopted them and they adopted us.

I soon discovered that Mama Bradford was a very busy woman. She belonged to all kinds of society clubs and social organizations. And she was involved in a lot of the Christian Science church activities, too.

Pops, on the other hand, was far less active in these goings-on. He worked long hours as one of the head-waiters at the Palmer House in the Loop.

In the meantime, Clarence never came to Chicago—thanks to the police officer and his woman friend and Aunt Irene. I believed I owed Clarence's absence to the New York postmark. So I began to relax, but I still had no interest in men. At the same time, Aunt Irene and Mama Bradford started to worry about me. After six months in Chicago, I still hadn't shown any interest in any of the men who'd tried to get to know me.

Christmas 1942. Mama Bradford and I went to Aunt Irene's for holiday dinner. It was a big family party. I enjoyed myself. Aunt Irene was not mad because I'd moved out. She understood. And this was the first of many such holiday celebrations I would spend at her home.

Soon after the holidays, one of my cousins intro-duced me to a man named Neil Houston, who was separated from his wife. Neil was a first-class decora-tor and was at that time redoing the inside of the syn-agogue at Forty-sixth Street. Neil was from Arkansas, but he spoke with a Geechee accent, like somebody from the Florida coast or South Carolina. He was nice and respectable, but he wanted to rush into a close, restricted relationship with me. And I wasn't ready for that.

Instead, I was now beginning to try to get a little

fun out of life, since I hadn't yet had much. Neil just didn't understand me. I mean, I hardly knew the man and he was already acting like a possessive husband—wanting to know where I'd been or where I was going. So I had to tell him that I liked him as a friend but that was all.

Then Enid introduced me to a fellow named Joe Trappe who'd just finished law school. Joe hadn't yet passed the bar exam. He was working as a waiter at a downtown restaurant. Joe told me he was divorced and had just lost his girlfriend. In fact, she'd suddenly married another fellow. But Joe was happy to have me as a companion to go around with. He wasn't trying to rush me into bed or into a serious relationship. And that was the way I wanted it.

My life was changing fast since I'd moved in with Mama Bradford and Pops. With Mama Bradford and sometimes without her, I was going to fashion shows and teas and fundraisers for charity. So I was having to spend much more money for clothing than I liked. But I was trying to learn how to be somebody new, somebody I could like without a second thought. At the same time, I was worried because my one-year promise to myself was running out and my savings weren't growing fast enough.

At the Nickel Spot, I had also recently met a man named Artie Jones. He eventually became a very important person in my life. Artie, like me, was white in appearance, and black by experience.

I really liked him as a friend. He used to stop at the Nickel Spot to pick up a quart of chili every Saturday afternoon when he was out on the South Side visiting his sister. He lived on Broadway, on the North Side, in a white neighborhood as a white person, but came to the South Side once a week, to see his black sister and her family.

Artie was originally from Texas. His mother was black and his father white. Going from colored to white and back was easy for him. He'd been doing it a long time. Artie always said, There's nothing behind whiteness and that's why it's so easy. If you look white you're white, he said. That's as exact as the law gets on the subject. Artie didn't even have to think about it anymore. In fact, it was easier for him to be white than black. Being black was something you were pretty much already conscious of all the time. To be white, Artie said, all you had to do was suspend Negro self-consciousness for a while.

Artie took me under his wing, showing me the ropes of how to get along in Chicago. He said, Inez, you have to use what the good Lord gave you. This is not a perfect world. In a perfect world it wouldn't matter if you were pink or brown, black or yellow. Everybody knows what kind of world we live in and what being white means and what being black means in that world. You're as white as any white person I've ever seen. Why not take advantage of that and get yourself a better job?

What was Artie saying? Was he suggesting I pass?

Pass my foot, he said. I don't call it passing. Most white people are passing, as you call it, they just don't know about their black ancestors. But you'd be surprised at how many of them suspect they have such ancestry. No, Inez, you'd be just doing what comes naturally with what you got. I bet you've had a hard enough time trying to be black, anyway. Haven't you? I nodded my head. I couldn't argue with him on that score. He said, Think about it.

And I thought about Artie's suggestion. Each time he came in for his chili he'd say, Are you thinking about what I told you? Yes, I was thinking about it, but that was as far as I'd gotten. How would I act as a white person? How do white people act? The more I thought about it, and the more I remembered the white folks I knew, the more I saw that there was nothing all that different in the way white people acted. Down home they talked pretty much with the same accent colored folks talked with. They laughed and cried the same way. I was thinking about it, but I wasn't ready just yet to take that step.

By June of that same year, 1943, Enid said I could take my vacation, so I could go and see you children. She paid me one week's vacation and gave me a hundred-dollars bonus. I called Lowella and told her I was going down home. Maybe she had a message to send by me to Mama and her boys. She did. And Artie picked me up, then we stopped by Lowella's.

She rode down with us to Polk Street Station. The last thing my sister said was that the minute I reached

Atlanta I should get a taxi and go straight to Mama's. In that way I wouldn't risk running into Clarence or having someone tell him I was in town. It was a good idea.

On the train that night I remembered my thoughts on the train leaving Atlanta: I would never again live with Clarence, and no man would ever again hit me. And now I prayed to get there safely and back. I prayed to be able soon to bring my children to Chicago with me. I prayed that I wouldn't see Clarence. I prayed for guidance. Then I went to sleep.

When I woke, I was in Atlanta and it was morning. I looked around. I was in a white car. Once again a conductor had seen me as white. He had not awakened me at the Mason–Dixon line. Maybe Artie was right. Maybe I could get a better job by simply *not* declaring myself a colored person. But would that be dishonest? I couldn't answer that question yet, but I was beginning to absorb some of Artie's way of looking at the matter. As I got ready to leave the train, a colored porter eyed me and I thought I saw him wink, but I wasn't sure.

The moment I stepped out of the station, a white taxi driver opened his car door for me, but I said no thanks, and walked around the corner to the "colored" taxi stop. Right away I got directly into a colored taxi. I told the driver—a thin, small old man with very black skin—that I wanted to go to Dublinville. He looked at me hard, then nodded.

Such a trip wasn't all that expensive. Outside city

limits, taxis cost fifteen cents a mile. On the way, I thought of Pa. He had had his second stroke, which left his left arm lame. The first stroke was in 1931. The driver was a quiet man. I tried a few times to strike up a conversation, but all he would say was yes ma'am and no ma'am. I wondered if he thought I was some sort of eccentric white woman who preferred to travel in colored taxis.

When I arrived, Mama came out to meet me. The driver watched as she and I embraced. I said to him, This is my mother. And he grinned and said, I sure was fooled. I said, What'd you mean? And he said, Nothing. And Mama just looked at him like he'd lost his mind.

On the porch, you and Serena were behind Mama, watching me, in that shy way of country children. I said, Come and give me a hug, both of you. And Mama said, What's the matter with you all? Go give your mother a kiss. She just came all the way from Chicago to see you. Then Serena came to me first and hugged my thigh.

But you hung back, still watching from a distance. Behind you stood Lowella's two boys, Harry and Philip. And Mama said to them, You boys remember your Aunt Inez. Come on and help her with her bags. And she reached back and pushed them toward me.

Pa was asleep. Mama said she'd see if he were awake. She knocked gently at his door and told him, Inez just got here. I was standing behind Mama. I heard Pa say, Tell her to come on in here and let me see her. Then I went past Mama into Pa's room.

Pa looked very old and weak now. He was confined to a wheelchair, parked at the foot of his bed. A geography book was open on his lap. He said, Come on in, Inez. I knew you were coming. I kissed his forehead. Good to have someone in the house with some intelligence, he said. And Mama—mumbling something in response to the insult—left us alone, closing the door as she left.

I sat down in the chair beside Pa. I sat with him a long while, asking him about himself, and telling him about my life in Chicago. Then, after a long silence, I said, Pa, I just want you to know that I love you very much. And I thank you for having been a wonderful father to me. I am grateful to be your daughter. He didn't say anything, but he reached over and squeezed my hand. Tears were in his eyes.

After I was there for several hours, you children warmed up to me. Serena showed me her pretty things and asked a thousand questions. She and you had grown a lot. You were still shy about talking directly to me. In fact, you'd gone off to play alone somewhere out back. I thought, Well, give him time. He was always a very sensitive and shy child.

It made me feel good to be with you children again. After the first day, I spent time on the front porch in the swing talking with you. Serena sat next to me and you sat on the steps a few feet away with Philip and Harry. All of you had a million questions about

Chicago. Do people live in glass houses? Is it true that everybody owns a car? Are the buildings tall as the sky?

The three of you boys talked from that distance, telling me about things you were doing. Every morning the three of you checked the rabbit traps Uncle Bert had set out in the woods. But once the newness of my presence wore off, you children went about your business in a normal manner, playing and working.

One morning after breakfast, and after you had gone outside, Mama said, Clarence wanted to know if you were a white lady. Mama had this quizzical expression as she waited for my response. I said, And what did you say? I told him, Your mother is not white, she's light, not white, light. Mama said she didn't think you understood the difference because you still looked confused. I thought of trying to talk about my color to you but decided against it because everything I thought to say sounded too silly in my mind. You were too young to understand this thing and I wasn't ready to tell you everything. I myself was still in the difficult process of accepting who I was and how I looked.

All too quickly my time was almost up. I began to feel the guilt again. I tried to talk with Mama about it, but couldn't get my words out correctly. I felt so emotional about it. You ain't got nothing to feel guilty about, Mama said. She said she didn't want me to worry about the children. Besides, she needed the money Lowella and I were sending her. It helped a lot. I stayed there four days and left on a Saturday morning—early, to catch that early bus to Atlanta.

I didn't stop in Atlanta on my way back to Chicago. But Mama later told me in a letter that your father came that Sunday. He must have somehow heard I was there. Even in small-town time, word-of-mouth traveled relatively fast, sometimes too fast. He spent a day with you all, then drove back to Atlanta. Mama said he pulled a loose tooth out of your mouth, and that a new one was already growing in.

Three months after I returned to Chicago, Artie stopped by for his chili and said, Inez, I found a job for you up on the North Side working in a nursing home. You are Inez, from the Deep South, with ancestors from Norway. Your family changed the family name to make it sound more American. Your family has been in this country for almost a hundred years, so you don't know a lot about your European ancestors.

I started laughing. Slow down, Artie, just slow down. Then he said, They need somebody right away. I told them about you. Mrs. LaFabian expects to interview you at nine o'clock tomorrow morning. Are you going to take the step?

I surprised myself. I told him yes. That evening, Artie coached me well on the rules of being white. We were having dinner together. The main thing, he said, is to be yourself. Remember, you do nothing special to be white. The trick is to act no different from the way you've always acted. Being white means being yourself. If you try to act a different way, you'll attract attention and people will think something is wrong with you.

I was there on time for the interview. Mrs. LaFabian, in a brown suit, was a kindly woman with a dignified manner. She gestured for me to take a seat in the old leather chair facing her desk. She herself stood alongside the desk balancing a yellow pencil between the palms of very dry hands with long, arthritis-twisted fingers. Tell me about yourself, Inez.

I told her the truth as I knew it. All about my growing up, even told her about feeling like an outsider, about my horrible marriage. I talked about my children, told her how much I missed them. The only thing I never said was that I was colored or Negro.

She listened with a sympathetic smile. When I finished she touched my shoulder and said, Well, I hope we can make you feel at home here. You will never be an outsider to us. We're one big family here. Today is Friday. You can start Monday. She told me my salary, and it was twice what I'd been making at the restaurant.

I quit my job at the Nickel Spot the next day. Enid told me to come back anytime I wanted to run the cash register for her. I didn't tell my cousin Enid what I was doing. I feared that she might not approve. Then I discovered that she knew about Artie. Enid came to me on her own and said, I'm glad Artie's helping you get a better job. She already knew.

So I quit to go to work as a white person in a white nursing home where no blacks worked. The home was in a strictly white neighborhood in the 1100 block on North Fairway Road, not far from Loyola University. Mrs. LaFabian herself was a registered nurse and manager of the nursing home.

Making the shift to being white was surprisingly easy. As Artie had said, it was no shift at all. I was myself—I remained myself. True, I was a bit nervous at first, but by the third or fourth day, everything felt as natural as it should. I hadn't changed. I was still the same. I had just moved myself out of one world into another. And now I was on my own.

Mrs. LaFabian said she needed me to help her with her two-story nursing home until her assistant, Floris Byczkowski, came back in six months from the WACs. Floris was her niece and she'd studied nursing before going into the army. Floris was stationed at a base outside London. Letters arrived from her on a regular basis. When something funny was in one of them, Mrs. LaFabian would read me the particular passage, and we'd laugh together.

I learned my job quickly. I answered the telephone and made calls for Mrs. LaFabian. I escorted visitors to patients' rooms. I recorded information that needed to be recorded in the patients' records.

But most of the time my duties kept me on the first floor, working closely with Mrs. LaFabian. Generally, I managed the office. I never had to go upstairs to help the nurses with any of the patients. The nurses liked

146

me and treated me well. We all lived there together, in separate rooms below the office. Only one of the nurses—Sheena—didn't like me. And I never knew why.

But without their knowing about it, I kept my room at Mama Bradford's, too. I told Mama Bradford and to my relief, she expressed no disapproval. I told Mrs. LaFabian I spent my day off at my sister's. And Lowella had the right kind of address, too, to back up the story. But I couldn't let Lowella come around, although she called me there.

Although this was by far a better-paying job, I was still worried about money. Staying with Mama Bradford—and being involved with her in her activities—I was forced to spend too much and not save enough. So, rather than going there on my day off, some afternoons I took the bus to Walton Place to visit Lowella.

She was a live-in housekeeper for a wealthy family, the Von Rummelhoffs. They owned a whisky distillery in Kentucky. Mrs. Von Rummelhoff's mother, Mrs. Charlesworth, lived with them in their mansion. The Von Rummelhoffs had lots of help, but Lowella was the only one who lived there. And she had lovely quarters—a little apartment of her own, on the first floor, in the back. The biggest part of Lowella's job was telling the day help what to do—and making sure they did it.

At other times, on my day off—and it was not always the same day—I met Artie, and he and I went out together, but not as sweethearts. Artie and I were never lovers. I loved him as a friend. He may have held romantic feelings for me. If so, they were not strong enough for him to try to pressure me into anything. He never once made a pass. We'd meet for dinner and take in a movie, or a stage show, or go to a nightclub to catch an act, then have a few drinks. I was not much of a drinker. I'd sip at one drink for hours.

Artie and I were being colored, as he put it, when we went out together like this. Now that I was being white in a natural way, I sometimes forgot that in order to shift back to colored all I had to do was just be sure not to change in any way except by thinking of myself as black. I had to keep telling myself that in the basic sense, I myself had not changed at all. Artie kept saying, Just be yourself, nothing except your surroundings has changed.

Years later—with my surroundings 99 percent black, and while I was living as a black woman—there came a time when, ironically, I had a hard time with my color. I was mistaken for a white woman running a business in a black neighborhood. It was 1968, during the Chicago riots.

When over the radio I heard an announcer say, Rev. Dr. Martin Luther King Jr. has just been shot, I dropped the jacket I was relining and rushed over to the radio. I felt cold and a fine sweat broke out on my skin and I was shaking. When I heard that King was definitely dead I screamed. My presser, working in the back, came to me and wrapped his arms around me.

I cried with my head on his shoulder. For me, King was the sign of hope in a lot of despair. His "I Have a Dream" speech had touched me deeply. In 1963 I watched him make it on television. His struggle felt like my own. And although I wasn't at the March on Washington five years earlier, I was there all the same.

My presser said, Don't worry, Miss Inez, his death is going to make him even more powerful. You think the Civil Rights Act was something? And now they talking about the Voting Rights Act. You just watch. Both of them ain't nothing compared to what the death of this man is going to accomplish. You just wait and see. My presser, too, was upset. I heard it in his voice. And he also knew, as I knew, that all hell was about to break loose.

The word spread fast. In an unconfirmed report, we heard that a white man had shot King. The word had already gotten around. Within a couple of hours, Fortythird was full of people. The presser went out to see what was going on. My clerk stood at the window looking through it.

When the presser came back, he said, At quitting time I'm gonna bring my car to the back door and we'll go out the back way, and I'll drive you home. Why the back door? But the minute I asked, I knew the answer. Because I looked white. And no white person was safe out there right now.

I kept looking out at the street and I was nervous. The crowds were getting bigger. By nightfall, I heard somebody out front shout, The gangs are gonna rumble *tonight! The presser then brought the car around. I locked up and made sure the cash register was empty and open. It was visible from the street through the plate glass. Then the clerk and I went out the back way and got in his car.*

While the clerk and I waited in the car, the presser turned on the alarm and locked the back gate. I had to make sure those things were done. He then dropped me off in front of my building. Then he drove the clerk home. She lived farther out.

Safe inside, it struck me that I'd just been driven home in my own neighborhood, a distance I'd walked hundreds of times on a normal day. Suddenly, for the first time in my life, because of my color my life was in danger.

In the days that followed, the gangs were organizing and planning to wreck the South Side. Everybody knew they were going to drive all white-owned businesses out of the area, set fires, loot, you name it. When older neighborhood people like myself asked gang members why they wanted to destroy their own neighborhood, they had no answer. I owned a small dry cleaning business on Forty-third near Cottage Grove.

The gangs were acting like units of an army—planning to hit a lot of different places all at the same time. I was outraged that they wanted to harm anybody, black or white. I had to know if Windy City, my shop, was on their hit list. A janitor who somehow saw the list told me, Yes, your place is on the list as white-owned.

I said, Didn't you tell them any different? He said he

wasn't supposed to have seen the list, so he couldn't say anything. He was scared of them. One of my customers, Pearl, was the mother of one of the gang leaders, a boy who called himself Geronimo. They lived next door to my cousin Ernest and his wife Ruby.

So I sent word to Pearl that I needed to speak to her son Geronimo. I'd known the boy since he was in diapers. She sent Geronimo to the shop. He came in looking sheepish. I told that boy that I wanted Windy City off that list. He looked embarrassed, but promised me he'd make sure Windy City was crossed off. It's just a mistake, he said.

Then I said, What good you boys think it's going to do—destroying your own community? I was angry. He gave me a blank look, then, stuttering, said, We got to do something, we can't just sit back and do nothing.

Every night before ten o'clock, all the white people were gone from the neighborhood. Some of them kept their colored managers in charge, others locked up and left early. These were places that normally stayed open late, sometimes till midnight, especially on weekends—liquor stores, drugstores, grocery stores and restaurants. Some of the white folks even sold their businesses to black people and stayed away.

But when the night of the big attack came, the gangs went along Forty-third breaking all the windows of all the shops. The gang leaders couldn't control the rioters. They weren't distinguishing between white- and black-owned. I guess they had no time to check a list. They hit every shop and stole everything they could carry.

151

Although the police had been alerted, they couldn't be everywhere at once.

The gangs broke glass and set fires. By morning, the street looked like a war zone. And it was the same all over the South Side. And from what I saw on the news, the same thing happened in all the big cities all over the country.

At times Artie and I went out as a couple of white people together, even sometimes pretending to be lovers, depending on the situation. He got lots of invitations to parties given by white people who never had anything to do with black people. In fact, we didn't know any white people who associated with black people. There were such people—mostly left-wing people or Communists—but we didn't know any of them.

Did I feel that what I was doing was wrong? No. I never for once thought that it was wrong. While living as white or black, I was able to see clearly that those labels had no real connection with real people, and that they were imposed from the outside, and that people either accepted them or rejected them. Although I lived both at different times, in my heart and mind, I rejected both.

During this time a doctor on Irving Park Road removed the gold crown from my front tooth and replaced it with a white one. That gave me my smile back. I liked myself in the mirror better now. At the dinner table that night, with the others who worked in the nursing home, I couldn't stop talking and laughing. I was happy to be rid of that ugly gold crown. And the girls laughed with me. But only Mrs. LaFabian knew the story behind the gold crown.

One day, Mrs. LaFabian told me about a program at Loyola that offered one of those evening courses for adults. She'd seen the ad in the newspaper. It was An Introduction to Business, a six-week course. I was interested and went and enrolled right away.

The professor was great. He taught us how to make budgets and how to figure percentages. He also taught us how banks figured interest rates. He taught us how to make a weekly or biweekly payroll on piecework. We learned how to keep records. We listened to the professor's lectures on business manners, on how to deal with coworkers and the public. Years later when I ran two different dry cleaning businesses, this training was put to good use.

After six months I left the employment of Mrs. LaFabian because Floris returned. But having worked there was a very valuable experience. I loved those people—the elderly, and the nurses, and Mrs. LaFabian. I felt great warmth for the old folks. They had seen me as only another human being. Being there, I learned that every moment of life was valuable. I also learned that while being white, the burden of race was lifted from me. And that was the greatest lesson of all. I'd learned the purpose of whiteness.

➤

We weren't expecting anybody when a knock came at the front door. I answered, and a well-dressed, slender black woman stood before me. Mama Bradford came up behind me. The woman said, My name is Nina Dobynes. She said she was looking for a room and had been sent by a friend of Mama Bradford's, Muriel Jackson. Mama Bradford invited Nina in and we sat in the living room. I knew Muriel washed hair in a Loop beauty parlor.

Nina explained that she worked as wardrobe manager for the comedian Imogene Coca. Coca was presently in a revue in the Loop. As it turned out, Coca had asked Muriel if she knew where Nina could find a room on the South Side. Because Nina was black, she could not stay downtown in the hotel with the rest of the touring company.

Mama wasted no time in renting Nina a room. Nina was poised as she talked. Mama Bradford and I had already heard that the famous comedians Sid Caesar and Imogene Coca were in town in a revue. Mama wanted to know about Nina's job. She said she bought clothes for Coca. She saw that they were properly altered and cared for. Nina traveled everywhere with Coca and helped her dress.

Years later, during the time when I was a full-time dressmaker, and when Nina was passing through Chicago with Coca, I did the alterations for the various new garments Coca was to wear on stage. She was good at standing still as a tree while I pinned the hems or sleeves.

And to make a long story short, Nina and I quickly became friends for life. When Sid Caesar and Imogene Coca started appearing in the television show *Admiral Broadway Revue* in 1950, the nature of Nina's work changed. She was not traveling as much as before. And the trips to Chicago became even less frequent when in 1954 the two comedians started appearing in the new TV show *Your Show of Shows*.

Over time Nina worked for other entertainers. At one point she worked for Danny Kaye. When for whatever reason Danny Kaye had to be in Chicago, I got to see Nina. I did a lot of alteration work for Danny Kaye's wife. On one of her trips to Europe Mrs. Kaye brought back for me a beautiful porcelain teapot as a gift of appreciation. I kept it in my dining room cupboard with my other precious things.

Although Nina and I didn't see each other often, we kept in touch by telephone. I'd tell her the details of my latest adventures. She in turn would fill me in on her travels to various cities in America and Europe. I loved hearing about her adventures in places like Paris and London and Rome. I thought she had the most exciting life of anyone I knew.

Eleven

Artie Jones had already picked up my things and dropped them off at the Bradfords'. The night before I left Mrs. LaFabian's, she and I sat up late talking. She told me not to worry. Things would work out for my children and me. I felt sad about leaving. Mrs. LaFabian and I had become friends. And now we were in tears over the fact that I was about to go. In the morning, I left after breakfast.

When I got off at Walton Place and saw the doorman at Lowella's, I started quietly crying again. I didn't know why the sight of the doorman brought on fresh tears. But inside, in Lowella's bedroom, I broke down and cried out loud. She tried to comfort me, but she didn't know why I was crying. In any case, Lowella had work to do. I told her to go and do her work. I'll be all right, I said. And she left me there and went about her chores.

I sat on her bed and cried. Although I had accidentally become white on the train going to Atlanta, the nursing home experience was the first time I deliberately did it for an extended time. I was accepted and treated well. I was discovering that whiteness was the ticket to more things than a better job with higher pay.

All my life, before then, in Georgia and Chicago, when some white folks knew I was not one of them, they often had not treated me as well as one of their own. And all my life, many colored people had treated me as though I was not fully one of their own. In both cases, I'd ignored the treatment and pretended that everything was fine. And it was because of my own lies to myself, about how I was being treated by blacks and whites, that I was now crying.

Sitting on Lowella's bed, I finally stopped crying. Lying there with my eyes closed, I could see now how things worked. Without colored people, white people couldn't be white and free of race. They needed colored people against which to achieve whiteness and the freedom that felt so good.

I finally slept and dreamt I was a child again with Pa, walking behind him, planting seed for trees. Pa was saying, These trees are going to grow up big and strong just like you. One day they are going to be taller than those big trees over on the other side of the road. I looked at the trees he was pointing to. They were the biggest things I'd ever seen.

Artie picked me up at Lowella's that night. He changed my mood. He kept me laughing all the way home to South Parkway because he was making jokes about colored folks and white folks, and the silly way they see each other. Then Artie said, Okay, Inez, get ready to be colored again. Just remember that the only change you make is not to change. That's the key.

Artie and I continued going around together a lot after I moved back to the South Side. At one white-only dinner party, the host, Katie Zarlego, met us at the door with her little white toy dog, Danta. He was standing beside her and wagging his tail. At the same time he was barking up a storm at us, sending a mixed message if I ever saw one.

Katie said, Come on in, you all, he won't bite you. And we walked in past the dog. When we got to the living room and were settled, as an afterthought, the host said, Danta doesn't like Negroes, but everybody else is okay. These words ruined the party for me. Artie just laughed. Comments like that didn't upset him. He always kept his cool.

Although I felt relaxed being white, and not changing, the sense of it was still new to me. Only once while working at Mrs. LaFabian's did I have to listen to a racial slur. One of the nurses, Sheena, said of one of the patients—an old woman, Mrs. Hazlitt—that her family down South once owned a hundred niggers.

And Sheena said, Niggers make me sick, you can't trust none of them. If you blink, they'll steal the clothes off your back. My husband, Ira, she said, keeps a gun in the house, and he says, If ever a nigger even so much as comes to our front door he's going to blow his head off.

Well, listening to Sheena, I was unable to hide how I felt. I couldn't help it. I said I was raised to like all people. I was never taught to hate, so I can't understand what you're talking about. And she just looked at me and finally said, You'll learn, just wait till you have to deal with a nigger. You've just been lucky so far.

A few days later, when I called Enid about my old job, she said the manager at the dime store down the street—formally known as Woolworth's Five and Dime—was looking for a clerk. I knew the dime stores hadn't yet started hiring colored girls to work the counters, so I was confused. I questioned Enid and she said, You passed for white on the North Side, why not out here?

And in fact Enid had already told the manager about me and he wanted to see me. I said, Did you tell him I'm colored? She said, No, but I told him you were my cousin, so I guess that's the same as telling him. Isn't it?

I was curious to meet a white man willing to hire a colored girl to work in a job reserved for white girls. Was he willing to hire any white-looking girl even if she was colored? The dime store job would pay me more than Enid could. But Enid said if I didn't like the job, I could always come back to work at the Nickel Spot.

At the dime store the manager escorted me back into his tiny office, and we stood facing each other. I suddenly felt shy but wouldn't let myself show it. The way he looked at me, I thought he was interested in my body. Then he said, I know you're a colored girl, but you look white enough to me. Enid is a good person and you come with her recommendation. If you want the job, it's yours. This is my little war against racism, he said. And I thanked him, relieved that I had misunderstood his eyes.

I was hired, but I worked there only three days. The manager introduced me to the four salesgirls working the counters, then left me in their care. Somehow they had found out that I was connected with Enid, and that I had actually worked in Enid's place. That, to them, of course, meant that I was colored. I had to be. I guess they assumed that no white girl would have ever worked in a place like the Nickel Spot.

Right away I saw that all four were going to be unfriendly. None of them spoke to me, or offered to show me the ropes. When I asked questions about my responsibilities, supplies and such, I got no answers. One filed her nails, another chewed gum, and looked off into the middle distance as if I had not spoken. I believed they were acting this way toward me because they believed I was not like them, and they didn't want a colored girl working on equal terms with them.

The manager had told them to train me and they refused, ignoring me instead. These girls wouldn't even tell me where to get the stock to resupply my counter. I finally told the manager that I couldn't work in that kind of atmosphere. And he shrugged, meaning that he was helpless to make his other girls like me. The fact was he just didn't care enough to hold them responsible for doing as he had instructed them to do.

So I walked out and never went back. And when I told Artie that I'd quit, he kidded me, saying, What'd you expect, you're colored again. If you'd gone in there as a white girl you wouldn't have had any problems.

I made up my mind to find my own job. I didn't really want to go back to work at the Nickel Spot. The pay was very low. I read the classifieds every day. I told everybody I knew to let me know if they heard of job openings. It could be colored or white. I didn't care as long as the pay was good.

And it wasn't long before I was hired to work in the kiosk at North Shore Railroad Station up on Howard Street. My boss there was Mrs. Geddes. This was not the kind of job they were giving to colored girls. That came two decades later. So on the job, once again, I was white.

Mrs. Geddes was a grim, short, stout woman who never said much. The day she hired me, she spent ten minutes telling me the rules and instructing me on how to run the cash register, how to keep a record of everything I sold—magazines, chewing gum, cigarettes, cigars, knickknacks. That was the most I ever heard her say at one time.

A day or two after I'd been on this job, a letter for me came to the Bradfords' from a lawyer in Atlanta. With it were the papers for a divorce, stating that I had deserted my husband and my children. I felt outraged at the idea. I was the one supporting them. Clarence hadn't contributed one red penny.

I called a lawyer, Joe Trippe, who used to eat in the Nickel Spot. I took him to dinner at Morris's. He'd always had a crush on me and I knew it. I told Joe the situation. I was angry and upset. He said, Sign the papers. Don't spend a dime. Sign the papers! You haven't deserted anybody!

I then called Attorney Jesse Hull, and he said, Bring the papers to me. I took the papers to him and he looked them over and said, Good riddance. Sign the papers! He said, The children are yours. They'll always be yours. This way you won't have to spend any money getting a divorce. So, sign the papers! Do what I say, he said.

Then Cousin Jesse Hull picked up the telephone and called Clarence's lawyer in Atlanta. He told him that his client had receipts showing that she alone had supported her children without any help from Clarence. Did that sound like desertion? It certainly did not. Cousin Hull told the Atlanta lawyer that his client had kept the children with her mother. He just wanted that lawyer to know.

So I signed the papers and put them back in the mail the next day. On paper, I'd agreed with Clarence that I deserted him and you children, and now he had custody. I was sure he was doing this to spite me, to try to hurt me in yet another way. But I knew him well enough to know that he didn't want you children. I wasn't worried a bit about losing my children to him.

I was now nervous and worried. Would he try to take you and Serena from Mama? That same day, I called the general store in Dublinville. Mr. Nixon, the owner, answered. I said, When Mama comes to the store on Saturday, would you let her use your telephone to call me? He said he would be happy to do it. And I gave him my number.

On Saturday, Mr. Nixon drove down the road, picked up Mama, and brought her to the store. When she called me, her voice sounded tiny and far away. But it was Mama all right. She said, What's the matter? Anything wrong? I said, No. Then Mama said, You worry too much. The children are all right, and don't worry anymore. Just hearing her say you were all right made me feel better. But I didn't tell her about the divorce papers. It was too much to try to talk about by phone.

While working at the Howard Street Station I met a good-looking man, Bill Kaminski. He bought his cigarettes from me—by the pack rather than the carton, which meant he came in often, sometimes twice a day. That's how I got to know him. He was two years my senior. Bill worked at an automobile sales lot down the street.

Bill was the first white man I actually dated while working as white. I didn't start dating him because I thought he was so great or because I felt a strong attraction to him. It was just that he'd come along at a time when, in my life, I felt alone and lonely. Also, he was not pushy, and he was interesting. Bill didn't send off sparks in me, but at first there was a level of comfort I felt with him in my presence and he in mine that made being with him better than just okay.

We did ordinary things together. Sometimes we walked along the lake. We went out to dinner and to movies together. Bill would stop to confess every time we came upon a Catholic church. I thought that was strange. It got to be awkward for me. Feeling silly, I'd stand in the doorway of the church, waiting for him. Sometimes I'd sit on a bench inside and look up at the graceful angels and saints on the red and blue stained glass. The churches were always dark and silent, except for the muffled sound of Bill's and the priest's voices, off to the side, toward the back, in the confession booth. Poor Bill, I thought.

He was a nervous talker and a chain-smoker. I, too, was smoking, but not like that. He'd been in the army and talked mostly about the good times he'd seen in Europe with his buddies, but I had trouble keeping focused on his war stories. And I didn't want to hear about desperate French prostitutes who were willing to do whatever he wanted in exchange for a pack of cigarettes. I soon realized that I wasn't really all that interested in his past life and how much fun he'd had. I was trying to get situated so I could send for my children. And when I tried to talk about myself, my situation, my life, my concerns, my hopes, he looked impatiently away, clearly not interested.

Only once did Bill make a reference to race. That was when a black man was passing in front of the car while we were waiting at a stoplight. Bill said, Wonder what they feel like being black like that? His voice was low. It was almost as if he were talking to himself. I didn't say anything in response. As we drove on, he started talking about the black soldiers he used to see in Paris with French women. He wondered what those women saw in black men. I still didn't say anything. Often I couldn't get a word in edgewise anyway.

Although I knew the relationship wasn't going anywhere, I continued to go out with Bill. Of course we went only to white clubs and movie houses on the North Side and in the Loop. I hadn't yet given him my address or phone number. I told him I needed to know him better before giving out that kind of information.

Then before long I learned that he was a weekend alcoholic. It happened when I called him at home one Saturday night. He was too drunk to talk clearly. Well, I thought, maybe he'd just had one too many. The next weekend, the same thing—stinking drunk and slurring his words.

It was on a Sunday afternoon. I met Bill at the station, which is where we always met when we were going out together. He arrived with bloodshot eyes, and he was staggering. That explained his usually red eyes and the unhealthy color of his skin. Right then and there, I just told him up front that I couldn't go out with him anymore, and that was the end of it. He gave me an apologetic look. I felt sorry for him. But I went right back up to the platform and caught the train back to the South Side.

When, several months later, Mrs. Geddes got her promotion and would not be there any longer, I left that job and went to work for a garment supplier named Sigelman and Fowlkes, Inc., which was across the street from the Chicago Theater on State Street. This was also a job reserved for whites only. My boss was Mr. Shackel, a man who never smiled. We filled orders from retailers.

Not long after I'd been on the job, Mr. Shackel told me that one of his customers wanted to hire me to work in her shop. In response, my first question was, Why did he want to get rid of me? He said he mainly needed order-fillers, and since I could sew and do trimmings, too, I'd be better off with Mrs. Kleinman. She needed somebody who could do those things. My talents, he said, were being wasted at his place. Also, Mrs. Kleinman was a good customer, and he wanted to keep her happy.

~

So, I went to work as a hat-trimmer in Lynn Kleinman's Millinery Shop on East Jackson Boulevard, near the Arthur Murray Dance School. Mrs. Kleinman had a well-supplied workroom and her hats were of fine quality. Most of the customers were regular and wanted their hats so individual in style that they would never meet themselves on the street. Mrs. Kleinman had no black employees, and I don't remember seeing any black customers, either.

Working in the Loop as a white person was easy. I wasn't likely to run into any colored people I knew. If I had, what difference would it have made? White people and colored people certainly talked to each other. But it never happened. And none of the white people I met in passing knew me except for those few who knew me only as an employee at Mrs. Kleinman's. In fact, I came to believe that white people were invisible to each other. In a crowd they noticed only black people. And black people mainly noticed only other black people. In effect, white people seemed not only invisible to each other but to everybody else.

Every day when I headed out to a nearby cafeteria for lunch, a middle-aged man was standing outside. He would follow me there. Once inside, somehow or other, he'd manage to get in line behind me. After getting his tray and food he'd follow me and try to sit at the same table.

After a couple of weeks when he finally spoke to

me, telling me his name, he started out right away talking politics. What we need in this country, he said, is a revolution of poor people, shop workers, bus drivers, people like you and me. Don't you agree? What he was saying didn't interest me, but I listened politely.

At other times, when I was at the counter waiting on a customer, he'd be standing outside the showcase window on the sidewalk watching me. He made me very nervous. Then one day he got up enough courage to ask me to come to one of his political meetings at the John Reed Club. He didn't have to tell me it was a Communist Party meeting. But I told him I was too busy.

In the meantime, I hadn't seen Artie Jones in a while, but I really felt I needed to talk with him about this persistent man who kept watching and following me. Artie had gone to Texas to see about some property he had inherited. And I really missed him. He'd taught me how to pass—or rather, how *not* to pass— and I thought I'd learned the rules, but what I had learned wasn't helping me now. Sadly, it would be many years before I'd see Artie again.

Then one day the man came into the shop and handed me some pamphlets and leaflets and a ticket to a banquet. After he left, I threw the papers in the trash can. In the days that followed, I changed my lunch place. Although I was now going in the other direction, to a fast-food hamburger joint, for a long time after that, I was still looking over my shoulder. But I didn't see him anymore.

I now had enough money in my savings account to get my own apartment, so I started reading the classified ads in the *Chicago Defender.* I marked off a few places each week and went to look at some of them, but every time I found something I liked, the landlord or agent told me I needed a man—a father or husband or brother—to cosign with me.

They all in effect said a single working colored woman with children is a bad risk. A colored woman couldn't get credit and she couldn't buy a car or rent an apartment on her own. I could see from observation that had I wanted to try as a white woman I would have been only slightly better off than as a black woman. I shouldn't have been surprised. Women hadn't had the vote all that long. But I refused to go along with their plan. No man would be living in my apartment, so why would I need one to cosign with me? And my anger just made me all the more determined.

Then came the big blow, in March 1945. One night Lowella called and said that she was taking the train home because Pa was dying. Pa dying? He'd been ill a long time, but I wasn't ready for his death. I felt physically ill just thinking about it. Anyway, I told Lowella that I'd get my ticket in the morning after the banks opened. I called my job and told them what was happening. And I got to Mama's only thirty minutes before Pa died.

As I sat at his bedside leaning over him, I could see that he was frail and slipping away. He was too far gone to know who I was. From my own perspective, this was the first death in the immediate family. Grandma Lucy died when I was thirteen, but she was not someone I saw every day like Pa, and besides, she was very old.

But I didn't know how to handle this death. I knew Pa was gone forever, yet I just walked around through the house in shock. I could not cry I felt heartsick. My whole body grew cold. I knew part of my world was coming to an end. I remembered our times together, remembered his teachings, his kindness, his love. And I was sick with grief.

Long ago, Pa had burned his insurance policies—thrown them in the fireplace—and told the agents never to come there again. Pa didn't believe in the philosophy of insurance. In his opinion it encouraged and fed on fear. So all of us had to pitch in on the funeral and burial expenses. But I didn't want to go to Athens with Saffrey and Lowella and Bert to make the arrangements, so I just put my share on the kitchen table. Wilbur was on his way.

I told Mama I would stay there with her and the children. You, Harry, and Phil were there, but Serena was now in Atlanta staying with her father for a while. Meanwhile, I heard that Clarence was telling people

171

that it was just a matter of time before I'd come running back to him. That's what he expected of me. Who could blame him? I'd certainly given him grounds for this assumption.

This time you were a little less shy with me, although you still didn't talk to me unless I asked you a direct question, and even then you responded only about half the time. I don't think you had started yet disliking me for having left you. That came later. Your anger, I mean.

The funeral home people fixed Pa's body up and dressed him in his dark blue suit, then they brought him in his casket to our living room where relatives and friends could pay their last respects before the burial. Seeing him dead and made up in the casket didn't help my grief. I just stood there gazing at his face and was still unable to cry. He didn't look like himself, but then I never knew an undertaker to get anybody just right. Who could expect them to? Most of them never saw the person when they were alive. I wanted to cry, but nothing would come out.

It was a big funeral. Pa was put away with dignity and a lot of sadness and tears. The cemetery was directly across from our house, behind Mr. Eddie Knight's cornfield. Bert and Wilbur and two Hull cousins were the pallbearers.

Clarence came, bringing Serena with him from Atlanta. I kept my distance from him and he kept his from me. We spoke politely to each other and that was about it. Serena stood at the graveside holding her father's hand and didn't look at me. I couldn't help but wonder if he'd turned her against me.

After the funeral all the family members left to go back home to Atlanta and to all the other various cities they'd scattered to. But Mama's sister Sara and I stayed with her. I wanted to be there to help Mama if she needed me, to help her get things in order, so she could go on with her life. And being there would help me do the same.

This was a slow time. Mama and I sat in the swing on the porch and talked a lot. Conversation ranged far and wide. We talked of the times when I was a little girl. She reminded me of how devoted I'd been to Pa. We talked about how I'd followed him around, step by step, helping him plant those trees that were now five times taller than I was.

More than ever before, I admired this woman who was my mother. Here was the woman who taught me as a girl how to be good and respected. How to set a table. How to make biscuits. How to hold my knife and fork when the preacher was over for supper and how to chew my food with my mouth closed like a lady. She was the woman who taught me how to wash dishes. How to clean house. How to make a bed. How to iron clothes. How to sew a buttonhole. How to sew a button on a blouse. How to wear a tampon when the time came. How to conduct myself around boys and men. How to sit on a chair with my knees together.

How to smile so people would like me. How to walk like a lady and not like a shameless hussy. She taught me how I was different from boys and why the difference was important.

Her lessons left me feeling that as a girl I was special. As special as girls may have been, they also seemed to be at a disadvantage when compared to boys. Boys had the freedom to run wild and to be themselves. At least, that was the impression I got watching my brothers.

While Mama set the moral example for my sisters and me, the manner of my conception and birth, in my later years, seemed in conflict with her teachings. She herself, though, had a moral logic that made sense to her. In her own eyes she'd done no wrong. When I was conceived her physical relationship with Pa had long since ended for good. Mama expected me to see the situation her way. And she expected me to follow the moral example she set as I was growing up. I didn't judge her. In looking back, my only disappointment was that Pa hadn't been my birth father.

I knew that Pa had raged against her in later years when he was confined to a wheelchair. In fits of anger he occasionally called her a floozy or a hussy. She knew and everyone else understood what was behind those angry charges. On the other hand, while I was growing up, he'd never made me feel unwanted. And during those years he never openly or indirectly spoke to her or to anybody of her affair with my birth father. In later years when he did start, she never dignified his attacks with a response. She kept her head high and her spirit high. She stayed calm and remained friendly toward him till the end.

Her memories of Pa were all good now. As we sat there in the swing she reminded me of the time I dug up four freshly planted fancy thin-shelled pecans and ate them. And Pa kept wondering why they hadn't sprouted. When he was about to write to the seed company over in Chattanooga to find out why they'd sent him seed that wouldn't sprout, I told him I'd dug them up and eaten them. Mama said, Pa just looked at you. You were grinning from ear to ear, she said. I hope you enjoyed the pecans, Pa said. They were extra fancy. Then I said, They were good, Pa, really good. And he just shook his head and laughed. I was a bit spoiled, I admit, but it was Pa's fault.

Day after day Mama and I kept on talking about Pa. She reminded me of how I used to follow him to the graveyard to clean his mother's grave. And I remembered Pa on those trips saying to me that when we cleaned old Nee's grave, that made her happy. She would be pleased with us.

Another time Pa and I planted a silver can with money in it for a rainy day. So every time it rained I would watch through the window, by the sage bush right at the garden gate, to try to see what would happen to our money. The memory of me doing that tickled Mama, and she just laughed and laughed.

Mama didn't seem to be grieving over losing Partner, as she called her husband. Maybe she saw his death as the easing of his burden. He'd been sick and in severe pain for more than twelve years. And in recent years, he'd been confined to a wheelchair. She'd had a hard time caring for him and keeping everything else going during those twelve years. At least in this way he was no longer suffering.

As much as I missed Pa, I was now looking at Mama, knowing that one day, if I didn't go before her, I'd have to suffer her passing on to that other place—

It was May 1980, when Saffrey's call came. She said, Inez, Mama just died. Come right away. I'm leaving for Dublinville in an hour.

I said okay and hung up. And I felt just numbness so far, but below that feeling, I also felt the rumblings of another layer of deep sorrow coming. I was going to cry, but it wasn't going to happen till later, probably after the funeral. But right now a sense of urgency and loss gripped me in such a powerful way that I wanted to at once fly up out of myself. I felt like my warm flesh suddenly turned to cold stone.

On the front porch Saffrey said, Mama is at the Hart Funeral Home, a mile and half east of here, in a place called Peach Harvest Point. It was new. When Pa died the closest funeral services for colored people was in Athens. But a lot of new businesses had sprung up all around Dublinville in recent years.

The next day we used the parking lot at the bus station across the street for all the cars. Sheriff Pete Kraft closed the highway above town and below the Hull house because there would be so many funeral cars moving in procession along the main road through downtown. Looking from the window of the limousine, at the closed shopfronts of Dublinville, I thought how much it looked like one of those abandoned and forgotten hamlets you can drive through sometimes on your way somewhere or nowhere in particular.

There must have been at least two hundred people in the family section alone at Mt. Zion Church. Looking around, I thought, People of all the different colors of the human race, in one family—my family. The flower girls were all great granddaughters. The pallbearers were grandsons.

It was grand. A Rev. Spencer K. Calhoun preached the funeral, calling it "The Rock of Ages." Throughout the sermon, he quoted various passages from Isaiah, Exodus, Philippians, and Acts, speaking of Mama's trust in God, her steadfastness, her devotion to her family and friends.

I closed my eyes and listened. A deacon named Brother Everett Parson made the remarks, speaking of courage in the journey of life. Sister Shannon Brown sang the solo, "Stand by Me." I didn't know them. And as I continued to look around at all the people sitting in the family section, I realized that most of them I didn't know, either, and had never seen before.

Now came the time of paying last respects. The immediate family went first. When I looked down at Mama in her casket, I saw a big woman—and she had been big for a woman—now shrunken to the size of a twelve-year-old child. She was ninety-one. Her face was hers, yet it wasn't hers exactly. The expression was wrong. And the line behind me, to see Ada Mae for the last time, grew longer and longer, so I moved on.

Mama was buried in the church cemetery right after the ceremony. And when the last shovel of earth was thrown on the mound of her grave, the tightness that had been in my throat all along got tighter. Although it was a warm afternoon, my hands turned cold. Back at the house, where food was spread out on every surface from the kitchen to the dining room, I kept looking at all the known and unknown relatives, and strangers, too, wondering who all these people were. I was looking at them through my grief like through a window clouded with steam.

I finally decided to investigate. So I started on the front porch with the idea of working my way into the house, and all through the house, back to the kitchen. I needed some answers. So I introduced myself to a big brown-skinned man leaning against the banister, holding a paper plate of potato salad and a fried chicken thigh.

He said, I'm Reverend Bronner. Now, I said, how are you related to me? We both laughed. I'm Albert Bronner's grandson. My name is Charles Bronner. I knew Albert Bronner was Mama's brother, the one my brother Bert was named after. Reverend Bronner pointed to a young man and said, That one over there is my youngest son, Ricardo. *My oldest boy, Harmon, is probably back there in the kitchen eating up all the fried chicken. And Reverend Bronner's shoulders rocked as he laughed at his own comment.*

A woman standing near us, listening to our conversation, butted in and said, your grandmama's sister was my grandmama. I looked at her. I knew Grandma Lucy had a sister, but I couldn't, on the spot, remember her name. I'm Gussie, the woman said. So she was Mama's mother's sister's granddaughter. Phew! Too many twisted connections to keep straight. I laughed. She did, too.

I moved on. And I kept introducing myself and meeting relatives of Mama's who lived all around this part of Georgia, people I'd never met before—older folks and younger folks, and the children of younger folks. But by the time I worked my way to the middle of the house— the dining room—I gave up on my investigation. Even if I met a hundred of them, how on earth was I to remember which name went with which face? And would I ever see any of them again anyway?

At this point, Saffrey pulled me into Pa's old bedroom and said, Nez, do you know that Bert wouldn't let me help with the funeral? He and that ex-wife of his, Arlene, and that adopted daughter, Nealy, selected all the flowers and the casket. And you know Mama never liked or trusted Arlene. I was so mad at Bert, she said. I don't know why he always got to be so evil. It just makes me sick.

And I knew Saffrey was telling the truth because Bert

was always contrary. If you said red he would insist on blue. If you said no, for him it had to be yes. Hearing this about Bert made me so mad I decided to leave and not stay, as I had planned, for a few days. My sister Brenna and her family were going back to Atlanta at midnight. We said our good-byes, did our hugging, then got on the road. If I had stayed, I would have told Bert off. But I didn't want to argue so soon after Mama's funeral. Bert sometimes acted like he had some sort of special right to Mama that the rest of us couldn't claim to the same degree. It really annoyed all of us when he acted that way. And he was at his worst with it right now.

Mama was in a talking mood. Eventually talk drifted away from Pa, but we kept talking. She reminded me of the time she'd sent me to the store to buy a slice of cheese. The grocer cut it like a slice of pie from a big ring sealed in wood.

As I stood watching him cut the cheese, Mr. Bean always gave me a thin slice to eat on the spot, but this time he was distracted and didn't. So on the way home, I pinched off a piece and ate it, and rewrapped it.

When I got home, Pa was in the kitchen with Mama. She unwrapped the cheese and took one look. Mama said she was going to take it back and tell Mr. Bean that rats had been in his cheese. Looking at Mama with big eyes, I said, I'm not no rat! Pa laughed, but Mama said, I ought to tan your hide. But Pa said, Ah, come on, Ada, the child didn't mean any harm.

And he laughed again. What I said sure did tickle him. And it wasn't the first or last time he defended me and saved me from a spanking.

Later that day, while Saffrey, Lowella and Bert were still in Athens, Mama and Aunt Sara and I were in the backyard washing sheets and blankets and rugs and scrubbing them on scrub boards propped up in big metal tubs. Mama had built a fire under the big black pot that sat down below the hedges and was boiling sheets. Aunt Sara was washing, and I was hanging the things on the clothesline.

In the middle of all this busyness, Mr. Eddie Knight stopped by to show sympathy for our grief. And it wasn't long before he reminded me that when I was little I was always up to their house. On rainy days, I'd watch for him to come to the watershed. When it rained too much to plow the fields that stretched out south of his house down to across the road from ours, and adjacent to the colored cemetery, he would go fishing. And he'd head toward the watershed when he got back and that was when I'd fall in step behind him.

I remembered some of those times. One time at the watershed he tied three turtle shells in a row on a string and made a train. He gave it to me as a present. I loved that toy and used to drag it around for hours. I'd drag it around all day unless somebody came and stopped me.

As we stood there in the yard talking, Mr. Eddie kept on remembering things. Another time he brought back an eel, but I called it a snake and he laughed. He reminded me of how I used sit on the floor at his mother's feet and listen to her stories. I used to stay with Mrs. Holly when I was too little to go with my brothers and sisters to pick cotton. I remembered her telling me about her childhood during the Civil War. I guess I was the only one who'd sit still long enough to listen to her as she sat in her rocking chair, knitting and talking.

Mr. Eddie then reminded us of the time when lightning struck our house and he and his daddy came down and helped us put the fire out. We threw buckets of water on it till we got the fire under control, he said, rubbing the corner of his eye. I said, You sure got a good memory. And he just wagged his head like a big old sheepdog. Then Mama changed the conversation by asking him about his wife. Mr. Eddie's visit was good for me because it brought back happy times. Right now, I needed a happy edge to my sadness.

The next day, I took the bus the ten miles to Athens to the funeral parlor to pick up the death certificate for Lowella. She had a small United Insurance Company policy on Pa, and she needed it to file her claim. When I got back, I went into Pa's room and called Mama.

I made a few suggestions for ways to make the room a little more useful to her. I said, Mama, you should let me redesign this room and get Bert to put that bed down in the cellar and—

She stopped me in midsentence, both hands raised. She wouldn't hear any of it. And I knew then that I should have waited. Pa hadn't been dead long enough for me to be talking to her this way. I was often like that, ready to move on, always looking to the future. Moving on didn't mean I wasn't in grief. But for Mama, I was moving too fast too soon.

She said, Pa built this house for me, and I'm not going to make any changes in his room. Well, let's at least get rid of the mattress, Mama. And to that she agreed. She and I threw out Pa's old mattress so that Bert could haul it to the dump. And the room smelled better after I opened the windows and aired it out all day. Beyond those changes, I left the room as it was.

Things stalled for a while. Before Clarence had taken Serena away with him back to Atlanta right after the funeral, I tried to take her aside and talk with her. But she wouldn't look me in the eyes. She was shy and didn't have much to say. I asked her about her life in Atlanta, asked her the questions a mother asks a daughter, the kinds of questions a father might not know to ask.

But she didn't want to talk. And I felt frustrated, then sad, then angry. And as soon as she could, she ran back over to her daddy. I was hurt but I tried, with all my might, to keep from crying or getting angrier. This incident made me all the more determined in my goal of getting my children back with me as soon as possible.

I couldn't say for sure that Clarence was deliberately turning my daughter against me. But Serena had never before been shy talking to me or to anybody. You had always been the reluctant, quiet one.

So, I now had two children who didn't want to have anything to do with me. At least, it felt that way. But I knew in my heart that it was temporary. There was no way that Clarence would be able to give you the kind of care I could and wanted to. The way he lived didn't allow for the kind of domestic life small children needed.

Twelve

I didn't stop in Atlanta on my way back to Chicago. Mama Bradford wanted me to talk about what happened. But I wanted to be alone in my room to just think.

Everybody was happy about the war ending and the boys in their pretty uniforms coming home, but my personal war was far from over. I felt bottled up. I had not yet cried over Pa's death. And at least on paper, I'd lost my children with the divorce and everyone said leave it alone, but I couldn't.

Meanwhile, I took my first airplane ride that year, 1945. Mama Bradford and I flew to Akron, Ohio, to visit her relatives for a few days. We saw boys in uniforms at the airport and everywhere. Up in the air for the first time, I was scared flying, but Mama Bradford was worse. She was so scared that she held onto her silver fox stole so tightly that she almost choked herself to death. And I was so busy trying to comfort her that I forgot about my own fear.

Another quick trip I took that same year was to St. Louis. I knew Sill Joplin from when I worked at the Nickel Spot. She asked me to go with her for the weekend, to hear a friend of hers from school days sing at the Key Club there. The friend was the singer Sylvia Johnson, who sang in her brother's—Buddy Johnson's—band.

I'd heard Sylvia's hit singles—"Please Mr. Johnson," and "When My Man Comes Home," and "That's the Stuff You Gotta Watch"—played on the radio and liked her singing. That year she was singing her hit "Since I Fell for You," and it had every girl dreaming of romance.

While in St. Louis, I remembered that old friends of my family, Frances and Norman Gillipan, now lived there. And I looked them up. They had both been close to Mama before they moved from Georgia shortly after Bert wrecked Pa's car and almost killed us all.

Frances was a hairdresser who later studied beauty culture under Madam C. J. Walker. So I decided I'd visit Frances and Norman while, in the afternoon, Sill visited with her friend Sylvia. She had some free time because Buddy's band didn't have to play a matinee anytime that weekend. I called Frances Saturday morning, and she said to come Sunday.

That left me looking toward Saturday with nothing to do. Saturday morning early, I ate breakfast at the Middleton Hotel, then sat in the lobby and read the *St. Louis Post-Dispatch*. Finished with the newspaper and bored, I went out front and got in a taxi and rode downtown to look for a movie theater. At the first one I saw I told the driver to let me out.

I later heard that the driver went back to the hotel and told Sill and her musician friends that he'd dropped me off at a white theater. The movie I saw was *Going My Way*, which was still playing in a lot of theaters, although it had been released the year before. I enjoyed Bing Crosby in that movie.

But I didn't notice till I was leaving the theater that there were no colored folks in there. When I entered, the theater was dark and the shorts were already playing. I took the seat the usher led me to and immediately became absorbed in the movie. I'd become so accustomed to moving both ways across the color line that I was beginning to do it without much thought.

I took a taxi back, and got out just before I reached the Hotel Middleton because I saw a restaurant. It was called Harley's Place. It looked pretty good, I was hungry, and it was near dinnertime. It was around five-fifteen. There were no other diners, although the sign on the door said dinner is served from five till nine. A pleasant, smiling elderly man I took to be Harley himself escorted me to a front seat by the window and handed me a menu.

Did it cross my mind that this might be an all-white place? Probably. Most places in St. Louis were segregated by race, black and white. You had to be one or the other. If you were black and from the right part of Africa, you might be accepted as white. But one thing you could not be was black with blood ancestors in America. Not even one drop. I knew all of this. So it must have crossed my mind. But, like I said, I was crossing the line so often now that I wasn't giving it much thought.

In short, my dinner of mashed potatoes, green peas, meat loaf and corn bread was delicious. And the waiter was a perfect gentleman the whole time. I finished and left a nice big tip. When I got back to the hotel my friend Sill and her friends were in the lobby talking.

They'd had a great time together and asked what I'd done. And I told them about the Bing Crosby movie and dinner. At this point they could have told me that I had gone to a white-only theater and eaten in a white-only restaurant, but they chose not to. Why they didn't, I can only imagine.

It was a tricky situation. If I was passing, then it put some distance between them and me. Maybe they thought I was deliberately and consciously passing, and if so, that showed me to be insensitive to them—insensitive because of the restrictions their colors placed on them. How could I say to them that I hadn't been fully aware that I was doing what they would have called passing? Who among them would have believed me?

There was also another thing involved in what I did. Neighborhoods in Chicago were completely segregated, but public places tended to be somewhat segregated. Like I said, after living in Chicago I'd gotten out of the habit of always thinking in terms of total segregation when it came to public places, such as theaters and restaurants.

Colored people in Chicago were free to go to any theater in the city even if they were encouraged to sit together, isolated from whites and honorary whites, such as—at that time—Jews and Arabs. This was done in an underhanded way. If you were black, the usher met you at the door and directed you with a flashlight to a seat. When you later looked around, you usually saw that you were surrounded by other black people and that you all were packed together into one area. This happened to me only when I was with another person who was obviously colored. It never happened to me alone, or when Artie and I were together.

But there were a lot of Chicago public places where black people were not welcome. It was not official, but it was understood. If you went into such a place, you were made to feel unwelcome. If it was a restaurant, you might be told there were no tables available even though you could see with your own eyes that there were tables, or you might be served contaminated food to encourage you not to return.

Sunday, when I came back from visiting with Frances and Norman, I invited Sill and her friends to go with me to the restaurant I'd discovered. That was how absentminded I'd become about crossing the line. The food, I told them, was better than the hotel food. And the place was within walking distance, right around the corner from the Middleton.

The minute we stepped inside, that same elderly man who'd seated me with a smile the day before rushed up to us with a frown and said, Sorry, we can't serve you people here. I looked around. The place was half empty, with plenty of empty seats.

We said, Why? He said, We don't serve colored here. I was truly surprised. I said, I ate here yesterday. He looked me over and said, We don't have a seat for you today. These seats are all reserved. I said, Then let me speak to the owner. He said, I'm the owner. I'm Harley. I looked at Sill and said, Can you beat this?

We turned and walked out. We were polite, though, although Harley wasn't. He slammed the door behind us just to make sure we got his point. No one said anything nasty to Harley, though we did look back at him and his mean face glaring through the glass door.

On the way back to the hotel, Sill said, Well, Inez, you got any more good ideas? Although I shouldn't have been, I was still shocked. And we all laughed. That's all you could do about such things. It was too stupid for words.

Back at the hotel we sat at the bar and ordered drinks. Alarmed by my own absentmindedness the day before, I told Sill and her friends about going to what was apparently a white theater. It was at this point that they confessed that the taxi driver had already told them.

After overhearing our conversation about incidents of racism we each had experienced at various times, the bartender said, Colored people bought this hotel only a few months ago, and certain places around here don't want our business. Harley's is one of them.

To me directly he said, Yesterday you were white, but today you are black. You went to a theater that doesn't admit colored, not even in the balcony. And I laughed. Everybody laughed. It was all so silly, painfully silly, but not new to any of us.

In the meantime, back in Chicago, another one of Mama Bradford's informally adopted children, Wesley Robertson, had come home from the war. Wesley was a good-looking young man with an almond butter complexion, dimples, curly hair and a thin mustache. He'd been in the navy in the Pacific and was at Pearl Harbor on December 7, 1941, when the Japanese struck.

Wesley was also on one of the warships that struck back at Japan from the Coral Sea. Besides Hawaii, he'd seen the Philippines and Australia, too. When he wasn't around one day, Mama Bradford told me Wesley was shell-shocked. But it didn't show except at night, when he sometimes woke up screaming from a nightmare. And I told her, I can't even imagine all he's been through.

I liked Wesley right away. He was originally from Kentucky. I told Wesley, Since I'm Mama Bradford's adopted daughter, that makes you my younger brother. He laughed, holding the palm of his hand out, and said, Put it there, sis. I liked his dimples. And he hugged me. Somehow or other, since I wasn't dating anybody and Wesley hadn't yet met a girl he liked, we kept each other company. We went out together on weekends to clubs.

Once Wesley and I drove down to Kentucky for his aunt's birthday. We danced at her party to Glenn Miller's music on the radio. I was not the world's best dancer and hadn't kept up with the latest dances, so Wesley was helping me with some of the new steps. I knew earlier dances, but by then people had stopped doing the Charleston and the Black Bottom.

Suddenly the music stopped, and the announcer said, We interrupt this program for a special announcement: President Roosevelt has just died. The room was instantly abuzz with shock. We were all stunned. People were saying, Oh my God, over and over. And when the shock passed, I felt sad—sad because Roosevelt was the first president that I really liked, without reservation. He seemed to care about poor people. He'd created jobs for a lot of them during the Depression—although, years later, I thought he would have been a greater president had

he taken a stand, early on, against racial segregation,
which he never did.

Anytime that I was enjoying myself or spending money, I felt guilty. I was still young and was trying to have some fun for the first time. And on the other hand, I couldn't stop thinking about my children and my responsibility.

Consequently, I went to church one Sunday and broke down and cried big sobbing tears. My whole body shook with pain. I hadn't known this was going to happen in a public place. I was in too much pain to be embarrassed.

Cousin Jesse Hull was a row over. He got up and came over and sat beside me and put his arm around my shoulders. And I lay my forehead against his lapel, but I couldn't stop shaking and crying. Yet I was grateful to him for being there, although I knew he thought I was crying over Pa's death. But I was crying over that and everything else, over the mess that I was in.

Although I was still scared and in great mental pain, by the end of the service I'd regained some composure. My cousin and I talked a bit while sitting in his car. He kept trying to comfort me.

I told him I was at a crossroads. I felt it. I could fall off the face of the earth or I could gain. There was no point in regretting anything in the past. The task now was to deal with the problems I faced and move on. Cousin Jesse approved of what I was saying. He placed his arm around my shoulder.

And I said, But it's easy to say these things, easy to *know* what I need to do. The hard part is *doing* it, I said. I knew that it wouldn't be easy to get up every day facing the rest of my not too promising life. Yet I had to do it. There was no turning back. For my children's sake and for my own, I had to keep going. My life didn't have to continue as it was. Things could get better than they'd ever been. That belief was so firmly rooted in me that nothing could shake it.

During this time my dreams were full of torment. In them I would fall down an embankment, but I'd wake just as the fall began. Each time this dream came back, it was the same way. I suspected it had something to do with my uneasy feelings about not having my children with me, not having enough money, and the uncertainty of the future. Yet I believed in what I wanted to do for my children and myself. And I knew my goal was in sight. I kept telling myself that my self-confidence and faith were growing each day.

Things stalled again for a while. Then, through Pops, I met Lola Whims. She had worked at the Palmer House's restaurant and had saved her money and opened a lunch cafe of her own on South Parkway across the street from the Regal Theater. Lola was a good example for me. I saw with my own eyes that a Negro woman was making a way for herself and her family. If she could do it, I could do it, and as a Negro woman.

Although it was just a basement place, with a counter and a few tables where she served lunch to walk-in customers, she was doing all right. The week-end matinees at the Regal gave her a lot of business because people stopped in, before or after the after-noon movies or stage shows. Entertainers like Billie Holiday and Cab Calloway, Count Basie and Duke Ellington, Pearl Bailey and Ella Fitzgerald were always appearing at the Regal and they attracted big crowds for the afternoon shows as well as at night. But Lola wasn't open at night. The night crowds went to restaurants on Forty-seventh Street.

Lola was doing so well that pretty soon she called me and asked if I'd help her out. She had more busi-ness than she expected. She did her own cooking with help from another cook, Mariah, who came in at six in the morning. I said yes, and went to work again as a Negro woman. I started at eleven to help with the serving. When I was done serving the noontime crowd, I worked till three on Lola's files. I checked out at three-thirty, and at four o'clock we closed.

Lola had one other waitress, Madeleine Grillet, a good-looking "yellow" girl from New Orleans, but Madeleine was a slow server. When she and I worked together, her drag-ass manner sometimes got on my nerves because half the time I was doing my job and hers, too. And Lola wasn't the type who pushed her help. In fact she used to say, slow or no slow, people liked good-looking women serving them.

Around this time a black woman named Mrs. Nellie Gankin, who owned a dressmaking and tailoring business on Wentworth Avenue, called late one afternoon to see if I could come and help her three evenings a week. She wanted me to help her instruct men and women on the GI Bill who were studying dressmaking at her shop. While still working for Lola, from 10 A.M. to 6:30 P.M., three or four days per week, I went to work for Mrs. Gankin.

Lowella, in the meantime, had moved in with her girlfriend Alicia at the new housing complex called Baby Doll Apartments on South Thirty-seventh Street. No question about it, I still looked up to Lowella as my older sister. And though I didn't always agree with her, I always respectfully listened to what she had to say. She had, after all, taken care of me when I was a baby. She had encouraged me to move to Chicago. It made me sad to see her now having severe breathing problems because of asthma, which she'd had for years.

Many mornings on my way to see her I'd stop by the drugstore and pick up her medicine for her. I'd take it to her and see how she was doing. Her latest doctor had recently discovered that in addition to the asthma, she also had a serious genetic heart condition. Upon this discovery he put her on a new medicine and almost right away she started getting better. That she felt better gave her some encouragement and made me feel good, too.

I didn't have a regular boyfriend at this time, but I was getting love letters every week from a man named Rufus Sims. I'd met Sims in 1943 at a political fundraiser for the Republican congressman Oscar dePriest, who owned the building the Bradfords lived in. Rufus lived down in Springfield and worked at the State House.

When Rufus came to town, he and I would go out together. We went to dinner or to a movie. Sometimes we went to Club DeLisa to see the chorus girls dancing, and to catch the comedy routines. At the time they were featuring people like Buck and Bubbles or Flournoy Miller, and traveling dance troupes with names like the Hot Chocolates or the Brownskin Beauties. I enjoyed these shows. Through their sense of humor about Negro life, and through dance expression, I was able to appreciate my own culture. When the comedians told jokes I was often reminded of Pa's great sense of humor. Black people had to be able to laugh at not just funny situations and ideas but misfortune, too, at life itself sometimes. Otherwise we would go crazy. Some of the jokes I'd already heard from Pa years before.

Then it was two weeks before Thanksgiving 1945. It started raining that afternoon while I was at work. After we closed, I came up the steps from Lola's to the sidewalk and it was raining cats and rats. I had a piece of newspaper over my head as I ran to the corner and waited for the Forty-seventh Street light to change.

And just then I glanced around and saw a very black-complected man in a suit and tie with a big umbrella running toward me from across South Parkway. Although I didn't know his name, I recognized him. I'd seen him before—in Lola's, I thought. He was all smiles. And he said, Hello there. Can I share my umbrella with you?

Thank you, I said. And in short order he started walking me south toward the dePriest building. On the way, he told me his name was Herb Darcy. Call me Darcy. Flashing me a gold-tooth smile he said, Everybody calls me Darcy. He sold new Buicks for a living. He said, I just come from backstage at the Regal. I was just talking with Duke Ellington. He wants to buy a car from me. I glanced at Darcy. He was looking smug and proud as he watched for my reaction.

I don't know why, but a week later, when Darcy came into Lola's, I asked him if he wanted to have Thanksgiving dinner with my sister, her friend Alicia and me at their place. He jumped at the chance. I was not sure of Darcy, so part of me probably wanted my sister to get a look at him, so she could tell me what she thought.

Well, I was surprised. Both Lowella and Alicia liked him, said he was nice. But I was still not sure. Although I was attracted to him, he seemed too slick. Something about him reminded me too much of Clarence in the early days before he started hitting me. My attraction to Darcy worried me, made me wonder again about my own judgment of men.

Darcy talked far too much about Al Capone—and he liked gangster movies. So had Clarence. Edward G. Robinson, Humphrey Bogart and James Cagney were Darcy's heroes. They'd been Clarence's, too. Darcy said he saw *The Last Gangster* and *Angels with Dirty Faces* more than twenty times. That worried me.

Another thing, Darcy also ran off at the mouth about the numbers rackets. That kind of talk scared me. And he talked about well-known underworld figures in Chicago, calling them by their first names, and that, too, worried me. So, despite my attraction, I wondered what I was getting myself into. Was it some compulsion of mine that made such men attractive?

No question about it, Darcy was nice to me. Against my own better judgment, I let myself get more and more involved with him. He'd come and pick me up, either at work or at Mama Bradford's, and drive me in his big new Buick any time of the day or night anywhere I needed to go. He showered me with gifts. And I was impressed by his fancy apartment, its bar and lovely furniture.

Little by little, seeing him became a habit. Then one day, Lowella and I had just come out of the post office, where we'd mailed our checks to Mama for the children. We were standing in front waiting for the streetcar when Darcy drove up. We climbed in, and he said he had a surprise for me. He proceeded to drive us to an apartment building at Forty-sixth and Prairie Avenue.

When we got inside, the manager said I could have the place, but I had to have a man sign the lease. Darcy said, I'll sign for you. I said, No thanks. You won't be living here, so why should you sign? The manager was watching us with a cynical smile. Who knows, or cares, what he was thinking. All I knew was that the requirement was against me. It was going to be the same anyplace I went looking for an apartment. I needed to figure out a way to get around the obstacle. Actually, I saw relief in Darcy's face when I said no. No way was I going to get myself under his thumb. I liked him, but I was not a fool. And I was happy to see that he didn't want to control me.

Mama Bradford made it clear to me that she didn't want me to move. She encouraged me to buy some new clothes to go with the new coat I'd recently bought, but I told her in no uncertain terms that my intention was still to save my money, to get an apartment and send for my children.

A few days after Darcy's attempt at a surprise, Mama Bradford tried to sell me a couple of tickets to an upcoming fashion show, sponsored by the Chicago Women's Trade Union League at the Parkway Ballroom. I turned her down flat. She didn't believe fat meat was greasy. I was determined to stop spending my money on such things. And I felt good about my new sense of resolve.

Being able to say no was new for me, but the more I said it to things I didn't want to do, the better I liked myself. And I felt stronger—better able to find my way. People always said, God will make a way, but I wasn't going to leave everything up to God. I was learning that I had to make my own way—and often make it where there was no way.

At Mrs. Gankin's, we the instructors didn't know anything about what was going on till the day it happened. Right after the first of the year, the government sent movers to the shop. In shock, we all stood up from our work tables. The drivers came in and took all her sewing machines and loaded them on trucks. They put us out and threw a padlock on the front door, then drove away with all her equipment.

I was stunned, but looking back, I knew I shouldn't have been surprised. On the bus home, I realized that I had been suspicious of Mrs. Gankin from the beginning. The signs were there, but I'd refused to read them for what they were.

It turned out that Nellie Gankin had a scam going. She'd been accepting government money for ex-GIs who were not actually taking sewing classes. Only about a third of the ex-GIs signed up were there in person. She'd sign these ghost soldiers in and out of classes just to keep her books looking proper. And she had been doing this since the end of the war.

Well, as a result, I was suddenly cut off from that salary, but I still had my waitress job at Lola's place and the tips were still good. I knew if I went full-time somewhere I'd have to give up the tips. Sewing was something I could easily do on the side. And I knew I was good, too. Once again, I read the classifieds and found something. I went down to Molly Kelly's, a dress shop on Michigan Avenue, and they hired me right away. At that time, they hired only white women. This would be part-time.

It was simple. In the sewing room, with other women who were also working at machines, my job was to hem dresses. I did some beading, too. This work, though, didn't take any imagination. As I worked, my mind drifted a lot. I liked the kind of sewing that allowed me to create interesting patterns or designs. This was a boring job, but I held on for about a month.

As usual, I talked by phone with my friend Nina Dobynes in New York. When I mentioned that I'd just quit the sewing job at Molly Kelly's, she encouraged me to come to New York to see if I wanted to try to make a go of it there. It would be great having you living here, she said, so I wouldn't have to wait till I come to Chicago to see you. And Nina knew I didn't dislike Chicago. Still, why not see New York? You might like it better, she said.

So I bought a train ticket for the Big Apple, and Nina took me down to the Garment District to look around, but I saw right away that I would not fit well into the sweatshop world. As I peeked in through the factory doors, I felt sorry for the women—a lot of them Chinese—packed in those places with their heads bent over sewing machines, for fifteen hours a day, working for peanuts. It was killing work. I'd never worked in that kind of sweatshop.

New York at the time didn't seem approachable, though I enjoyed my visit. Yet Nina kept trying to talk me into moving there, but my mind told me that Chicago was my best bet—especially for bringing up you and Serena. I knew Chicago, liked it, and had lots of friends and relatives there.

Shortly after I got back, another newspaper ad led to my next job. It was a women's clothing shop owned by J. Desani-Seervani. I didn't have to be black or white with Desani. The minute I laid eyes on him, I just knew.

It didn't matter—maybe because he was not born in America. Desani was about forty, short and stout, with very dark skin, and straight black hair. His first name was Julian, but since he didn't like his given name, he told everybody to call him Desani, one of his family names.

Although born in Bombay, Desani was now an American citizen who'd come to America young and broke. At first he sold cosmetics door-to-door to get started, then set up his own cosmetic business, and then got married. Just before I went to work for him, he'd changed from cosmetics to garments.

He was now separated from his wife, Gita, who also ran a dress shop out on Fifty-first. They were still friends and she'd stop in Desani's shop from time to time to see how things were going. She, too, was from India. At first I liked her.

Right away, Desani and I felt that we had something in common. We both had stomached failed marriages, and had had to make a way out of no way. Here we were now, trying to make some money to help put our lives on track. In that shop, Desani and I became a successful two-person team.

It was at this time that Lowella's boy friend, Thobias Johnson, came out of the army. Right away, I liked Thobias. He was three or four shades darker than Lowella, and stocky, with arms that looked like he'd been lifting weights. In almost no time, Lowella and Toby got married. They moved into an apartment on Forty-sixth Street and Vincennes Avenue. Soon after the quick and simple wedding, I remember going over there for Sunday breakfast.

During breakfast Lowella banged her water glass on the table and suddenly spoke in a harsh tone to me. She told me she was sick and tired of me with my head in the clouds. She said she'd changed my diapers and knew a few things more about life than I did. I was silly, she said, thinking I could get an apartment on my own, and bring my children to Chicago and be a one-parent family.

Chicago was a rough city, she insisted, and a woman alone couldn't properly raise two children here without help. She said, The kids are better off where they are, Inez. Why do you think I leave my kids with Mama? Isn't that right, Toby? And of course Toby agreed, as he poured more syrup on his pancakes.

Well, they'd both spoiled my appetite. After her outburst, I only picked at my food while respectfully listening to the rest of my sister's quieter lecturing. When she was done, all I said was, I know you have my best interest at heart, Low, but I'm still sending for my kids, and I'm going to do all I can to bring them up by myself. All I can do is pray that they'll turn out all right. But there's nothing you can say that's going to stop me.

She then said, a hard head makes a soft behind, Inez. Sure, I knew that expression. In fact, Mama used to use it. Anyway, my feelings were hurt, but I was not angry with my sister and my new brother-in-law. Although I wasn't hungry any longer, I politely waited till they finished before leaving the table. And soon after that, I left their apartment just as determined as ever to carry out my plan.

Mama sometimes wrote long letters telling me what she and the children were doing. Depending on the season, she was doing one thing or another, making soap in a big black kettle out in the backyard, canning fruits and vegetables for the winter. You children had your chores. When Serena was not in Atlanta with your father she helped Mama around the house and in the kitchen. You boys checked the hen nests for fresh eggs. Daily you still scouted the woods checking the rabbit and opossum traps set by your Uncle Bert.

You chopped and brought in wood for the stove and fireplaces. You weeded the garden. You gathered ripe figs and apples and pears from the trees surrounding the house. Mama always made it sound like you were having a great time. But still I worried that you and Serena were not as happy as you could be with me. And I beat my fists against my bed at night trying to figure out a way to make it happen without delay.

Thirteen

So for a year I worked at Desani's and tried to save my money. One evening in early August when I got home, Mama Bradford gave me a message. A woman in Winder, Georgia, had called and left a telephone number asking me to return her call.

Even before Mama Bradford told me the woman's name, I knew it had to be Miss Anna because I knew she had recently moved to Winder to stay with her oldest daughter, Estelle, who was now a preacher like her mother. I remembered Estelle's dimpled smile during the time she worked with me at the Piedmont. I wasn't surprised when I heard she'd given herself to preaching the gospel. She was always so serious and so driven.

I was supposed to call at seven o'clock the next night. I did just that, and the white woman Miss Anna worked for answered the phone, saying, This is the Burnwell residence. I told her who I was and she said, Anna is waiting to talk to you.

Then Miss Anna said hello and she couldn't get the rest of her words out clearly for crying. She blew her nose and tried again. Miss Anna told me that Clarence took you children from Mama and brought you to her. She said, This happened two weeks ago. Then Miss Anna said that her daughter Estelle had beat you for keeping a stray dog tied up in the backyard.

She said, Clarence found a dog. That first night the dog started whimpering. Estelle got sick of listening to it, and she got up and went out in her nightgown. She untied the rope from the mutt, then she came back in the house. She got her husband's razor strap from back of the door, and started beating your son Clarence in his sleep.

Miss Anna said, Inez, she beat the boy within an inch of his life. And your son is suffering with asthma, too. I'm afraid for the children in Estelle's house. Please, Inez, Miss Anna said, don't tell nobody I called you. I would be in a whole lot of trouble.

Well, that did it for me. Clarence had moved you children from Mama's to spite me. That was clear. I didn't care what the divorce papers said. My children were mine. Ready or not, I had to take action. I told Miss Anna that I was sending for little Clarence and Serena right away. I felt a fury rising in my chest. I told her that in the meantime she should find a big box and put the children's things in it, and ship the box to me COD, and she said she would.

When I hung up, I turned and looked at Mama Bradford, who was standing behind me. Tears clouded my eyes, blurring her. I said, My children are going to be with me next week. She sighed. You got a place for them? she said. Yes, I said, they're going to stay right here with us. I'll pay you for their room until I get a bigger place. I'll pay you extra to use the kitchen, too.

And Mama Bradford just stood there giving me her skeptical look. Finally she said, I don't want the extra money. What she wanted, she said, was for me to take off from work to help with the housework, and to look after the children, and to clean up after them until I found a place. And since I didn't want to argue with her, I didn't respond. It was a silly idea. How could I manage without working? Instead, I picked up the phone and called my boss, Desani, and told him I'd be late the next day.

The minute I hung up from talking with Desani, I sent my sister-in-law in Atlanta a telegram. In it, I told Carrie to get in touch with Clarence right away and tell him to get the children from his sister's house and bring them to her. Tell him I said that the children are coming to Chicago to live with me.

Then I wired the train ticket money to Carrie, so that her oldest son, Joseph Allen, could escort you and Serena to Chicago. Joe was about seventeen and you were too young to travel such a distance alone. After that, I called Cousin Jesse and asked if my nephew Joe could stay with him and his family for two or three days. No problem, he said. After all, Joseph was a Hull. It would be good for Joe to meet his successful relative the lawyer. I knew, too, that Cousin Jesse had strong family feelings.

But I was a nervous wreck for the next few days. I couldn't be still. I smoked one cigarette after another. I paced the floor. I couldn't sleep. I couldn't stop talking. One day, on my way home during this waiting period, I stopped at the Ritz Lounge, in the Ritz Hotel at Oakwood Boulevard and South Parkway, to talk with the manager, Hank Miller.

He smiled a lot, with two front teeth capped with gold that flashed like camera light. I knew him through Darcy. I also knew through Darcy that Hank often got places for musicians gigging at the lounge, so he knew a lot of landlords and landladies, knew of vacancies.

Hank knew everybody and knew about everything going on. I asked him if he knew of a vacant two-bedroom apartment that I could rent without a man's signature. He said no. I said, Okay, let me know if you hear of anything.

Just as I was about to leave, Hank called me back. Wait a minute, he said. He picked up the desk phone and said he was calling a house across the street. He talked with somebody he called Chuck. Hank said, Come on over, I'd like for you to meet her.

In five minutes, the man called Chuck came walking into the lobby and Hank introduced us. Charles Peterson was his name. A slow talker, he said he and his wife, Rebecca, owned that big house over there. He pointed through the plate-glass window and said we got rooms and apartments we rent out, but we don't have nothing right now.

Hank said, Inez is good people, Chuck. She's got two kids and she needs a place. Can't you and Becky do something for her? Chuck scratched his head. Then slowly he said he had an apartment that was going to be vacant in three weeks. But we don't want any kids in there, he said. And I felt his eyes on me as he talked. He was now looking me over, inspecting me. And, disappointed, I just looked back at him.

The next day, soon after I got home, Becky Peterson herself called me and asked me to come down to see her. I took a jitney down and she greeted me on the front porch. Becky was a good-looking light-skinned woman with a fluttery and regal manner and lots of makeup. She and I hit it off right away.

In Becky's living room we sat and talked. She said her cousin, Earlie, was presently living in the apartment in question but that he was leaving in three weeks, going back to Nashville to stay. Earlie don't like Chicago, she said. She said, I'm willing to let you have the apartment with your children, if you'd be willing to let an old lady stay in the back room. I hesitated to say anything in response. I needed to see the place first.

Her cousin was out at the moment, so Becky took me upstairs and showed me the apartment. The living room was small. In its far corner was the intersection to the rest of the apartment. We walked over there and stopped. To my left, I could see into the first small bedroom. It had one window. Before me was a small kitchen with a skylight and no other window. Straight ahead, through the kitchen, was the other, bigger bedroom. We walked through the kitchen and stopped at the doorway. This bedroom was twice the size of the first one, and the room had two windows.

This was the room Becky wanted to rent to an old woman. The old woman would have to come and go through my apartment., I didn't like the idea, but I was desperate. So I said, Sure, I guess that would be all right. The way I figured, this arrangement wasn't going to be for long. I would keep looking for a bigger and better place. The point was, I needed a place right now. And this would be an apartment where I didn't need a man to cosign with me. So I said okay.

In short, Becky called the old woman. Her name was Miss Nola Stonebank. She lived a few doors down the block. Miss Stonebank came twenty-minutes later and we met. She was shy and soft-spoken, a plain woman in glasses and a green cotton dress, and she wore her bluish-gray hair pulled back in a bun. I liked her right off. She'd worked as a maid at a hotel in the Loop for twenty years before she retired. She had a grown son and daughter, and her husband was dead.

Later, Becky told me she and her first husband bought the house, and now her second husband, Chuck, wanted to run it and her, too. She wasn't about to stand for it. He'd advised her not to rent to me because of the children. She laughed and said, He goes around telling everybody that this house is his. I just smiled. Then we talked about the rent, and it sounded reasonable. I offered her a deposit, but she refused to take any money from me. When you move in will be soon enough, she said. And by the time I left Becky's house, she and I were good friends.

After that arrangement, I had a lot to do in a short amount of time. The first thing I did was to put a down payment on some furniture. I would have to pay thirty-two dollars and fifty-two cents a month till the bill was paid off. I also paid for two metal cabinets and two gallons of off-white paint at a Thirty-ninth Street hardware and had the store hold the order for delivery till after Earlie moved. The store owner said when I was ready he'd also send me a man to paint the apartment.

Step by step, I was getting there. I then bought pots, pans, dishes, glasses, silverware and a tablecloth. Serena and I would sleep together while you would have a single bed to yourself alongside us. My dream was for each of you to have your own bedroom, but right now that was not possible.

The big day arrived. Darcy drove me to the train station at Polk Street to pick you up. Darcy and I stood at the gate watching. I was nervous. When I first caught sight of you, I was amazed by how big and tall you'd grown in less than a year. You were nine and Serena was eight. I couldn't believe my eyes. Since Pa died, Serena had grown to almost twice your size. And my nephew Joe had sprouted legs so long he looked like he was walking on stilts.

Driving back to Mama Bradford's, I kept turning around looking at the three of you, shy and quiet in the back seat. I kept asking questions about the train ride and everything else I could think of. And I kept getting one- or two-word answers. Then I noticed that you were looking vacantly out the window with your mouth slightly open. I said, Clarence, close your mouth, honey.

You looked surprised, but I felt motherly. Holding one's mouth open for no reason showed a lack of breeding. And pretty soon I'd be saying sit up straight. Use this fork, not that one. Tie your shoes. Comb your hair. Brush your teeth. Serena's hair looked like it could use a good brushing. I was ready to take charge.

As we neared the dePriest building, despite my happiness, I was also suddenly scared, scared that I wouldn't be able to handle the situation, scared that I wouldn't be able to make enough money to support us. What if I lost my job? What if I couldn't find another job right away? What if I couldn't pay the rent? Buy food? What if I got sick? What if one of you got sick and needed hospital care? I had no medical insurance. What would happen to us? What if I couldn't get you to obey me? What if you got into trouble? What would I do? What could we do?

It was true that I might be able to find a better job as a white woman somewhere in the Loop, but I could not and would not let such an effort cause me to deny or hide my children. It would be more difficult now with children if I went back to working white.

214

In the 1940s it was not common to see white women with children of obvious mixed race. There were a few, of course. If a white-looking woman was seen with colored children, she herself was assumed to be colored. Forty years later that was no longer necessarily true.

But now I had to be strong. As Darcy drove us home, somehow I managed to put my fears to rest—at least for the time being. After Darcy left—he didn't stay long—Mama Bradford got to know you. For a woman who hadn't been around children much, and one who had already indicated to me that she wasn't about to become my nanny, she warmed up to you right away. Seeing this was a relief because her flat was where we would be, at least for the next three weeks.

The following day, I showed you children around the neighborhood. You seemed happy to be with me, and I was grateful. While we were walking up South Parkway, my old fear of not being able to make it hit me again. I remembered hearing about a place on Archer Avenue where single women with children to support could go for financial assistance. I really didn't want public support, but I thought it wouldn't hurt to find out what was involved. It wouldn't hurt to know what a person needed to do to get it, if an emergency were to arise.

So a couple of days later, with birth certificates in hand, I took the streetcar to the building on Archer Avenue. An elderly white woman was behind the counter. I told her why I'd come. She looked me up and down and said, What's wrong with you? You're young and intelligent, and in obvious good health. Why can't you support yourself and your two children?

I couldn't answer her, and I walked out feeling ashamed of having given in to my fear of not being able to make it. On the streetcar back home, I decided I would not be a beggar. I never liked the idea of public assistance anyway, except in emergencies. I had simply to get a handle on my fear and move ahead. I already had my plans in place. Now I needed to keep my courage up.

Meanwhile, I had a lot to do. When I got home, Mama Bradford was having fun. Serena had on my lipstick and high-heeled shoes, and she was clomping around with her fist propped on her little hip like she was Mae West. Under normal circumstances, I would have laughed right away, but it took a moment, and even when I laughed, my mind wasn't on laughing.

That afternoon I heard the vegetable wagon coming through our alley on its usual route. I grabbed my change purse and ran down the steps to get out there before the vegetable man passed.

He'd seen me anyway and was pulling his old nag to a stop right by our back gate. Other women were now coming out also and heading for his wagon. A couple of men were there already. One of them was the neighborhood numbers runner, Jellybean Johnson. I said, Hi, Jellybean.

When I finished shopping, Jelly carried my bag of vegetables upstairs for me. And while Jelly was taking Mama Bradford's numbers, I fingered the pages of his *Prince Ali Lucky Five Star Dream Book* and found "fears." Each idea, activity, place, person or thing— such as "bride" or "cats" or "umbrella" corresponded to a particular three-digit number. "Fears" corresponded to the number 771, and because of the type of dreams I'd had lately, I played 771—not that I fully believed in this lucky dream stuff. Jelly took our numbers and our two dollars and wished us luck.

Early that evening he came back with four hundred dollars for me. He said, Miss Noz, you're a winner! My three numbers won? I was beside myself with joy, despite the slight sense of guilt and shame I felt for having gambled. Having won meant I now had money for the rent without having to go into my post office savings. I couldn't stop talking and moving about. I hugged the children. I hugged Mama Bradford. Jelly and Mama and Pops all tried to get me to play again, but I said no. But I couldn't help thinking how so much in life was a gamble.

I told them I wasn't a gambler. And I said, Like an old lady down south used to say, the Devil might have brought the money, but God sent it. They all laughed. And after that, whenever Jelly came knocking on the back door to collect numbers, and we'd call out, Who's there, he'd laugh and say, Open the door, it's the Devil!

I had to get you enrolled in school. That was my next step. I went to talk with the administrators at the

217

Catholic school. It was supposed to be better than public school, but it was going to be too expensive. Besides, you children told me you didn't want to go to Catholic school. You'd heard that the nuns were mean and that they beat your knuckles with rulers.

So, that next Monday, I enrolled you in Forestville Elementary Public School, which was a big redbrick, three-story building that took up a whole city block, only five or six blocks away, at Forty-fifth and Forestville Avenue and St. Lawrence Avenue. You and Serena would be able to walk to school in ten minutes. But I was worried about you getting to and from school safely. I remembered my own troubles and how I'd needed a bodyguard when I was your ages and younger.

Kids fought after school, and sometimes even before school. Playground bullies were a natural part of the scene. So were the victims, but I didn't want my children being victimized. I knew you were not bullies. I was worried that other children might pick on you and Serena because you were new and talked with southern accents. Plus, Clarence, you were quiet and sensitive, and I knew that that combination was a magnet for bullies.

My children would not have somebody like Blake with them to keep the bullies at a safe distance. Also, Chicago was not Dublinville, nor was Forestville David T. Howard in Atlanta. Forestville was a bigger and rougher school in a bigger and rougher city.

Yet I knew I couldn't be there to protect you all the

time. Children did tease you, saying things like, Is that white woman your mother? How come your mother is so white and you so black? If that lady is your mother, your daddy must look like a baboon.

You and Serena didn't like my going with you, but I made it a habit of walking with you to school before taking a jitney down to Thirty-fifth, and walking over to Desani's shop to work. At three o'clock, when school let out, I was right there waiting for you.

I kept this up a long while. Serena, especially, was embarrassed for her new friends to see her white-looking mother escorting her and her brother. But sure enough, a bully had threatened you at lunchtime, though he hadn't yet gotten his hands on you. And the biggest and baddest girl had pushed Serena in the hallway a couple of times, trying to start a fight. Still, so far, nothing serious had happened.

In the meantime, at PTA meetings I met some of the other parents and got to know your teachers. Then one day Serena told me not to meet you anymore. She would take care of herself *and* her brother—as if you were the youngest. She was, after all, much bigger. I wanted to know why she suddenly felt so safe. Or was it just that she felt embarrassed? No, she explained. The day before, during lunchtime, she'd whipped the biggest and baddest girl in school, and now nobody was ever going to bother her again.

Fourteen

It was October. In the middle of the third week after your arrival, Becky Peterson called and said her cousin was about to move out. We could get ready to move in. I called and had the paint delivered, and the painter finished the job in a day and a half. The next day Miss Stonebank moved in. We followed the day after.

Right after the holidays—to catch the sales—Darcy was driving me down to the Loop to Goldblatt's Department Store. On the way, at Roosevelt Road, a white policeman pulled him over. The officer came to the car, bent down, and looked in, taking a close look at me, and said, Are you all right, ma'am? Are you okay?

I said, What do you mean? The officer turned red in the face and said, You know this man? Does he work for you? I said, No, he doesn't work for me, he's a friend of mine. What's the problem, Officer? Just checking, but you seem to be all right, he said. We've had reports, and I just want to make sure everything is okay.

After the officer left and Darcy drove on, Darcy laughed and said, You know what that was all about, don't you? I said yes. But I was angry, and I couldn't understand why Darcy wasn't even angrier than I.

When Darcy and I walked through Goldblatt's together—or when we went anywhere together beyond the South Side—white people stared at us, turned around and looked. It was happening now in Goldblatt's.

One of my defenses was to avoid eye contact. I had become accustomed to this sort of thing. I no longer tried to imagine what they were puzzling over. Let them figure it out for themselves. The lady with her driver? A white hussy with her big black lover? I knew the line of thought: she couldn't be a self-respecting white woman, had to be a tramp, a lowlife whore. Who else would have anything to do with a black man?

I bought pillows and pillowcases, sheets and blankets—enough for two changes for the three beds. I paid cash for these things, with my own money, not Darcy's. The only help I was accepting from him at this time was his kind willingness to sometimes provide me with transportation.

When the clerk and I finished with the paperwork, Darcy suggested we go downstairs to the basement in Goldblatt's and buy some food. He offered to pay for the food, and reluctantly, I let him.

That night Wesley and his brother Nelson helped

me move my things from Mama Bradford's. In the process of moving, I felt the old fear again. Most of the money I'd saved was gone for one thing or another.

The sense of independence I sometimes felt, and wanted to go on feeling, seemed to be slipping away. I was now in deep debt. I knew that meant more worry and troubled sleep and sleepless nights.

You children quickly got into a routine. You didn't have to transfer from Forestville, at least not right away. You took the bus and it cost a nickel each way. You caught it at Oakwood and South Parkway and got off at Forty-fifth and walked the three blocks over to Forestville.

On weekends Wesley was an usher at the Park Theater—called "the dump"—on Forty-seventh Street, which specialized in westerns and comedies. He'd told me to send my kids to him on Saturday afternoon while I was working at the shop. He let you in free, and kept an eye on you during the double and sometimes triple feature of movies starring Hopalong Cassidy or Tom Mix or Abbott and Costello. You always came back excited about what you saw. You were especially excited about the cowboys and the horses. You wanted one of your own. I kept telling you it was not a practical idea, but my words had no effect on your fantasy.

Soon after we moved into Becky's house, Chuck took off for Los Angeles, taking with him a young woman called Dixie. Where Dixie came from no one knew.

Becky was heartsick over her second husband's leaving, and wanted to talk with me about her troubles every night when I got home. I was tired and had to make dinner. But I politely listened each night for as long as I could.

When it was clear to her that I didn't have time to be her bosom buddy, she started selling dresses and hats on commission. She got a percentage of each sale. She'd sit in her picture window, like a New Orleans whore in the old days, and tap a quarter on the glass when she saw a likely customer going by. These would-be customers were neighborhood women, coming and going.

Sometimes when Becky had a fresh shipment, she'd stop me on my way in and hold a dress up against the front of my body. She'd tell me how great it looked. She'd want me to try it on, then and there. But after she built up a list of customers, she started working mainly by appointment. There were times when I was glad to get in and out of the house without having to look at the pretty dresses and hats.

Everything was fine till the middle of January, when we started getting a bad odor in the apartment. I kept all the windows opened trying to get rid of it. You were feeling sick and so was I. It was getting worse, and after a day or two—in the middle of the night—I discovered that the secondhand refrigerator I'd bought just before we moved in was leaking gas. I immediately unplugged the thing. At first light, I got two men from the gas station on the corner to carry it down to the porch.

Later that morning, Becky got somebody to take it away. I called Desani and told him what happened and that I'd be in later. Then I took the el down to the Loop, looking out the window at all the dilapidated apartment buildings along the way, and feeling grateful that we didn't live in one of those dark, decaying tenements. Even in our situation—not much money and living in a crowded apartment—there was something to be grateful for.

I was also grateful to have accomplished my goal of getting my children up to Chicago with me. It was a culmination, a turning point. Now a new, stronger self was being reborn somehow out of the ashes of that self that struggled so long to reach this point. And I liked my new self better.

I bought a new refrigerator at Goldblatt's on credit. By now I had a good credit record. And for the refrigerator I'd have to pay eight dollars a month. I believed in my heart that I was not poor. It was something I repeated to myself often. And I carried myself as though I had everything I needed and more.

They were bringing the refrigerator out the next day, so when I got to work at eleven, I told Desani that I'd have to stay home to receive the delivery, because there was a COD charge of thirty dollars. He said all right, and closed the shop, and went off to a luncheon with three men from India. It was an overcast day and nobody was coming in, anyway.

225

When I got to the shop later, I sat on the stool behind the counter with a notepad on the countertop. I took a pencil and started working on my budget to see if I could make ends meet. I was still very worried about money, but so far I hadn't asked anybody for help—not Clarence, not my relatives, not the public, not Darcy.

While I sat there I heard on the radio that President Truman had just gotten a raise that brought his salary up to seventy-five thousand a year. When Desani came back, I mentioned this to him and said, I need a raise, too. After all, while he was the owner, I was president of the dress shop. He laughed at my joke. Desani said, All right, sure, I'll give you a two-dollar a week raise, Miss President.

And so he did. That brought my salary up to thirty dollars a week. Desani said that that was more than any other clerk along Forty-seventh Street was making. I certainly didn't know what people were making, but I was happy to get the raise. It boosted my spirit.

When I got home from work one evening you were lying on the couch. You said you didn't feel well. I took your temperature and discovered you had a fever. You said you'd been playing out front with the two boys who lived next door. They were the sons of Dr. Miles Howell. I knew the family, but only in passing. Amelia and the doctor also had a daughter, the youngest of the three.

The next day you had red blisters on your back and

chest and upper arms, so I took you next door to Dr. Howell's office. Chicken pox, said the doctor. He gave me lotion to rub on your skin, and big white tablets for you to take. Four days later, Serena broke out with the same kind of blisters. I called Dr. Howell and he said, Give her some of Clarence's medicine.

You all stayed home from school till you were over the chicken pox. Then when you were back in school, I, too, came down with chicken pox. Miss Stonebank helped me during this crisis. She had helped with you before, and now she even rubbed the lotion on my back, where I couldn't reach.

But she and Becky didn't catch it. They no doubt had had it as children and were now immune. As a result, I lost a few days' work, but at least when I went back, I was happy to see that Desani hadn't caught chicken pox from me.

Becky was busy these days, with lots of company. Many of the musicians who were playing nights at the Ritz Hotel's lounge and the nearby Southway Hotel's lounge gathered in her living room to socialize. The ones working at clubs in the Loop also stayed out south during the day.

Becky was usually renting rooms in the basement or on the first floor to these men, and they all knew her. Most of them did not have big public reputations, but were just hard-working and hard-traveling musicians, working in well-known bands. They were men who had worked with people like Count Basie or

Duke Ellington, both of whom Becky called her friends because they had, at one time or another, rented a room from her.

Becky had a grand piano in the sun parlor, and a vibraharp always sat against its far wall. She said Lionel Hampton—who then lived in California—left it there so he'd always have it to play whenever he stayed with her. She said he was originally from Kentucky but had grown up in Chicago, playing drums in the *Chicago Defender* Boys' band, and she'd known him a long time. During the day, the musicians rehearsed, playing the piano and the vibraharp, and some of them sang. Sometimes I'd come home to a festive atmosphere, and had a hard time getting through Becky's place to the stairway upstairs because everybody wanted me to join the party. Most of the time I was too tired, but I didn't have the heart to walk through without at least stopping for ten minutes or so. Becky was always there in the center of the fun, having a good time. Seeing her that way was how I wanted to always remember her.

It was sad when, many years later, I had occasion to visit a nursing home. A very old woman who looked slightly familiar met me at the entryway and said, Welcome to my home. And I was sure I knew her voice and her face, but I couldn't quite place her. She gave me an uneasy feeling as she paraded around me in the lobby as if showing off her living room.

She was dressed like a bad imitation of somebody

ready to go to church on Easter Sunday. Her makeup looked like a small child's work—a red circle on each cheek, and red lipstick smeared over and around her lips. She wore tons of powder all over the surface of her face. It clung to her eyelashes. But I quickly realized that she was a resident patient and that she wasn't about to go anywhere. Ironically, this was her home.

Then I looked closely at her eyes. She was still talking, talking nonsense, and I was still looking at her eyes. It then came to me. This was my old friend Becky—Rebecca Peterson. Seeing her like this was a shock. And it brought back memories of the Oakwood house and the way Becky was then, and Mrs. Stonebank in the back room of my apartment, and the other people I knew then.

Just as I was about to tell her my name, she broke away from me to go to greet two other women just then entering the lobby. Stunned, I watched her greeting the women with blustery charm, gesturing toward the lobby, inviting them in. She clearly hadn't recognized me.

The two women ignored her and kept walking toward the reception desk. They no doubt had encountered her before. Then Becky came back to me and said, How do you like my house? I bought this beautiful place in which to entertain all my friends, she said. As she spoke she was waving her hands toward the ceiling.

I said, Becky, I'm Inez. Don't you remember me? She kept smiling and said No, I don't believe we've met before, but you're welcome in my home. I said, Thank you. And I told her I'd see her later. Well, although she *wasn't aware of it, this was the second time she'd made me welcome in her home.*

Then I went on to the receptionist. I asked about Rebecca. And the receptionist said, Oh, Becky, she's in good health, physically, but her mind is gone. She doesn't remember any of her relatives or friends. She's been here a year now.

The receptionist continued, Unlike the other patients, Becky gets up early every morning and dresses herself without help. She goes to breakfast by herself. She's no trouble. Nobody has to clean her. She knows how to use the toilet.

The receptionist then laughed. The funny thing is, she thinks we all work for her. In her mind, this is her house and we are all her servants. We let her welcome the guests until after lunch. It wears her out, and after lunch she takes her afternoon nap. It works out fine for us, the receptionist said. Tears came to my eyes as the receptionist talked. And I turned away so that she couldn't see. But later, I laughed at the absurdity of it. And still later, tears came again.

During this time, Forestville Elementary School sent me transfer papers because we had moved out of the district. Before this notice I hadn't known for sure where the district lines actually were drawn. In any case, I was instructed to enroll my kids in Wendell Phillips Elementary School on Thirty-ninth Street at 244 East Pershing Road. So right away I got you both transferred, and Serena adjusted well.

You, at this point, lost interest in school. Years later you told me one of your favorite writers, Nella Larsen, who wrote books about women like me, had attended Phillips back in 1905–1907. Despite your poor performance there, you came to feel proud of that connection with Larsen. But in the meantime you'd just adjusted to Forestville and you didn't like the change. A few weeks later your new math teacher sent me a note saying that you were failing. If you didn't improve; she was going to fail you.

So I hired a tutor, a high school girl, to work with you. And she helped a lot. And you improved and finally passed math. The girl also taught you how to use the Oakwood Public Library, three blocks east on the corner of Oakwood and Langley, and after that, you started going there on your own, often. You would bring stacks of books home and you would sit and read them one by one. In fact, you read so much I began to worry that you were not exercising enough.

Meanwhile, I missed Artie Jones. The number I had was disconnected before he left town. Thinking he was back by now, and that I might be able to reach him by mail, I sent a postcard to the only address I had, and it came back stamped *Moved—No Forwarding Address.* I called his sister's number, but that, too, had been changed. She now had an unlisted number.

Our precinct captain—Jackie Tucker, a Democrat who owned a building about seven or eight houses east of us—wanted me to pitch in and help him get people registered to vote. Because I believed in what he was doing, I agreed to help as much as I could.

But Jackie's car had stopped running—stopped for good. I told him Darcy would give him a good deal on a new car. Then I told Darcy about it and he handed me the paperwork. So I filled out the contract for Jackie. He was getting it for one thousand two hundred dollars. I'd given Darcy the tip. I made the transaction. I did the paperwork. In other words, I sold the car. So that night after the deal was done, I asked Darcy if I could have part of the profit. But he refused, saying he owed all of it and more to the automobile company. I didn't believe him, and even if it were true, I thought that was unfair. His refusal soured my view of Darcy's honor.

It was around this time that Lowella got upset with me because when I changed my address, I also changed my political party from Republican to Democrat. Usually I had voted Republican without thinking much about it, but after living in Chicago for some time, it seemed to me that the Democratic Party stood more for working people like myself than did the Republicans. In the South, back in Mama's and Pa's day and before, colored folks voted Republican because Republican President Lincoln freed the slaves.

Also, the Republicans had tried to do the honorable thing for Negroes after the Civil War, and during Reconstruction. Everybody knew that. Besides, most of the white folks in the South were Democrats, and not many of them had the Negroes' interest at heart. For most black folk down home, that in itself was enough reason to vote Republican. So Lowella was mad at me once again, and this time I didn't care. This was a new day for me and I was moving forward with a changed mind.

Fifteen

So I started helping Jackie Tucker in what little spare time I had to get people in the neighborhood registered to vote. We couldn't tell them to vote Democrat, but we did our best to get them to the point where they could choose.

Then—as if I didn't have enough trouble the old gas stove in our apartment started leaking gas. Every time I turned the oven on, flames leaped out at me. Since there was a leak, I didn't want to risk burning down the house, so I went back down to Goldblatt's and bought a small apartment-size stove. I had them put it on the account with the refrigerator. Becky got a couple of men to move her old gas stove out to make room for my new one.

Money worries still had me climbing the wall, because I was in far more debt than I had ever planned. I worried and couldn't sleep well. Sometimes because of night worry I got up to go to work with only two or three hours sleep. But I told myself to keep on keeping on. And I didn't give up. Where there was persistence, there was a way.

It was the middle of April, just before my birthday. I came home from work and was in the kitchen cooking spaghetti and hot dogs when I heard a knock at the door. I thought it was one of my neighbors from the hallway coming to borrow something like salt or sugar. When I looked into the living room, one of you children had opened the door and there stood my ex-sister-in-law Estelle.

I was shocked. She was standing there with a stiff, dimpled smile. I took a few steps into the living room but made no attempt to touch her. In my immediate family, two people who hadn't seen each other in a long time always rushed to hug, and maybe even kiss. I am sure that her family was like that, too. But she and I just stood our ground. I noticed that you had stepped back from her and were standing now between Serena and me. I said, Have a seat, Estelle. I couldn't control the sudden unnatural tone of my own voice.

She walked over to the couch and sat down on the edge. And with a nervous smile she said, Inez, I just stopped by to see how you and the children are doing. I'm on my way to Portland for a sanctified revival meeting. She was nervous, but she kept her smile. She said she was changing trains in Chicago. I then politely offered her dinner. But she said no, that she'd eaten already. Then I offered her—and she accepted—a glass of lemonade.

I thought I had forgiven Estelle for the cruel beating she'd given you, but at that moment, seeing her then, I realized I still held anger. I actually had to put forth extra effort not to tell her how I felt. She'd done a mean thing—brutally beating a child while he slept. And for what? Because a dog's whimpering woke her.

Estelle didn't stay long. When she asked me to call her a taxi, instead I got one of the roomers downstairs to drive her back to the station. When he got back, I offered to pay him, but he wouldn't take any money. That night Serena told me more details of the beating. I felt sick. Although Estelle lived for many years after that, I never again saw her. She died in Anniston, Alabama, where she spent her last years, near where her father, George Major, and her grandfather Ned Major were born, at Smiths Station in Lee County. Estelle and her preacher husband had gone to Anniston and established a church, which was what they did in each new place they came to call home. They were a migratory family.

Shortly after Estelle's visit I came home from work one evening, and as I approached the house, I saw Becky hurrying down Oakwood in an agitated manner. It was already dark and the streetlights were on. I waited at the front walkway. When she was within speaking distance she said, Serena's nowhere to be found. She threw her arms up. I've looked everywhere.

I took a deep breath and tried to keep calm. We hurried into the house. I wanted to see what you knew, to find out where and when you last saw your sister. I found you on your knees, building a city inside a cardboard box. You were worried, too. The last time you saw Serena she was going off with other girls toward the Ida B. Wells Projects, a big housing development one block over on Thirty-ninth.

I didn't like you kids to go there because there was too much trouble you could get into. But all the kids from all around were attracted to the Projects because there was a playground with swings, a rec center, a running track, a football field and a swimming pool.

I knew the three girls Serena played with most often—Tanya, Yvonne and Carlotta. All three were around her age and lived on Oakwood down the block, Tanya and Yvonne on our side, and Carlotta on the other side.

Usually the four of them jumped rope out on the sidewalk, or played hopscotch. Or they sat together on the front steps of our house, or on the steps of one of their houses. And they read comic books, or just sat around talking girl talk and eating candy. They chewed gum, seeing who could blow the biggest bubble before it popped.

Come on, I said, Clarence, let's go find her. And our first stop was at Yvonne's. She said she hadn't seen Serena since they came back from the Projects around five-thirty. It was now after seven. At Tanya's house we heard the same story. Then we crossed the street and knocked on Carlotta's door.

Carlotta's mother opened the door, and with a big

smile said, I bet you're looking for Serena. And over her shoulder I saw Serena and Carlotta sitting on the living room floor, looking at the screen of a small television set. But Serena had turned around the moment she heard my voice. I saw televisions in department stores but even rarely there. This was my first time seeing one in someone's home. I was sure this was Serena's first time watching a TV. She'd obviously become so captured by the magic box that time slipped by without notice.

And soon after this scare, I bought a little television set from Elliott, a plumber and radio repairman down the block. But not much was on the TV, except on weekends we saw Sid Caesar and Imogene Coca. Yet Serena liked having it in the house. You still liked best the weekend radio shows, *The Shadow*, *Boston Blackie* and *The Fat Man*.

We didn't have much time during the week to talk together. On weekends, though, we did talk. Conversations varied. Once you wanted to know what I was like as a child. What did I play with? Did I ever steal anything? My answer was, there was nothing to steal. We talked about the books I insisted you read. When I asked you about your schoolwork, I rarely got the kind of answer I wanted. But we were never at a loss for conversation when there was time to talk.

Soon Mama sent a letter asking if she could have the children with her for the summer. I asked you two how you felt about it, and you said you would like to

239

go. Nevertheless, I suspected that you weren't all that excited about the trip, except that it would give you the opportunity to see your father. You, more than Serena, were keen on that aspect of the trip.

So I sent you at the end of June and you stayed six weeks in Dublinville, spending the final week in Atlanta. I also wanted you to have an ongoing relationship with your father. In fact, I never spoke against him to you. For your sake, I felt I had to put my troubles with him aside. From my point of view, the summer was uneventful, and my children came back suntanned and a fourth of an inch taller.

A short time later, Nina Dobynes came to town. Her theater company was performing at the Chicago Theater. I couldn't put Nina up, so I reserved a room for her across the street at the Ritz Hotel. As before, because of her color she couldn't stay in any of the big hotels downtown with the rest of her company. It was humiliating being the only backstage worker who had to go off and find a room elsewhere because of her skin color. But I was so glad to see Nina, and happy to have her staying just across the street. It meant I'd see more of her.

She hadn't been in Chicago in quite awhile. The last time, Nina stayed in an empty room at Mama Bradford's, and we did a lot of going around together. But this time—despite the fact that a room across the street was registered in her name—I saw very little of her. She was working almost constantly. She had both matinee and evening shows to attend to.

She still lived in New York. Keeping in touch with her helped to give continuity to my life. I'd lost contact with Artie, a valued friend, and with a few others. I was also far away from most of my relatives. But I was determined not to lose Nina. She and I were so much alike in many ways: independent and hard-working. She also had two children. We understood each other.

We had breakfast together at the hotel a few times, and once we went shopping together in the Loop. She had a list of things she needed to buy for her show people. I mainly went along just to get to spend some time with her. I liked and trusted Nina because she had always been open and direct with me, and I'd always felt that she wanted nothing from me but friendship. I was sad that we had so little time together.

Sixteen

After working late one night, I came home and the minute I stepped into the apartment I smelled a horrible mustiness. I looked in the bedroom and you children were asleep. I turned on the light in the bathroom. The bathtub was dirtier than I had ever seen it before. My comb and brush had long black hairs in them. They were not human hairs. An empty can of flea powder sat on the ledge of the face bowl. Suddenly I noticed that the bathroom was full of jumping fleas.

Back in the living room, I saw that the couch was damp and so was the rug, and fleas were jumping everywhere. They had to be fleas. I knew fleas when I saw them. In the kitchen there was one of my good bowls on the floor, half full of water. Beside it, in a plate, was the bone left over from one of the steaks I was saving for Sunday dinner.

I ran back into the bedroom and turned on the light. The first thing I noticed was a big rope tied around the post at the foot of the bed. Clarence, I said, Clarence, you may as well get up, boy, and explain what's going on here.

Serena stirred and pulled the cover over her head. I heard the dog moving around under your bed. As I was talking, the mutt stuck his little face from under the bed with the spread draped over his head like a shawl, and he looked up at me with black shinning eyes. Then he crawled out and stood up, still watching me. I could see that he was only a few months old. He was the same black color as the hair in my brush.

I felt heartsick. I was too tired to be angry. I felt like crying. I opened the door and called Becky upstairs. I wanted to know if she knew anything about this mess. She knew, all right. Being a dog lover, she hadn't seen anything wrong with you claiming yourself a dog, one that obviously needed a home. In fact, Becky laughed at my distress. She laughed so hard she wet her pants. And I ended up both crying and laughing with her. But nothing—believe me!—nothing was funny.

Becky went back downstairs and brought up a can of flea spray that she kept for her own dog, Missy. She was an old black Labrador that was mainly interested in eating. When Missy wasn't eating, she was warbling around until she found a comfortable place to sleep till the next feeding time, when she'd pull her old self up to walk to the food bowl.

Becky also kept a parrot in the kitchen. She called her Polly. Polly talked a lot. Mainly she said, Polly wants a cracker. But she'd also hear a phrase such as something one of the kids said, or something I said, and a few hours or a day or even a week later, she'd repeat the phrase, word for word. One such phrase for a while was, Roy Rogers and Trigger! Roy Rogers and Trigger!

Anyway, that night, after I got rid of the fleas and cleaned up the apartment, Becky talked me into letting you keep the dog. I remembered how cruel my ex-sister-in-law had been to you when you'd tried to befriend a dog at her home in Winder. I couldn't be the second one to deny you something you wanted so much. But I untied the rope and took the dog down to the backyard and tied him to the banister. I would not have a wet flea-ridden dog sleeping in the house.

In the days that followed, you called the dog Black Jack and enjoyed playing with him till a week later, when he was run over by a car right in front of the house. I got the story when I came home from work. Becky told me she'd given the dog a burial place at the end of her garden, which was on the left side of the house behind a large billboard. You held a funeral, with neighborhood children joining you in your grief.

Later I walked around to the side of the house. I looked at the little wooden marker you had made and stuck in the ground at the head of the grave. I could tell you were sad about the loss of Black Jack, but I also saw that you were going to be all right about it. You just needed time to get over your grieving.

A couple of days later Desani said he wanted to train a young woman from India to be a salesclerk, so he asked me if I'd go to Gita's shop and work with her while he was doing this training. The young woman, who was called Kirin, actually had already worked as a salesclerk in Desani's ex-wife's shop. But I wasn't told this at the time. The truth was that she had had an argument with Gita and left in a fit of anger. Unaware of any of this, I agreed to go to work in Gita's shop at Fifty-first and South Parkway.

What a mistake! Gita was a disagreeable person. She had no price tags on anything and her shop had no regular customers. Her prices, which often came off the top of her head, were too steep for the neighborhood. If a woman came in and tried on a dress, it would usually not fit. The first time Gita told a customer, Inez will shorten it for you, I knew Gita was just trying to use me. I wasn't there to do alterations. That was not in the agreement.

Gita had a pushy personality and a bad attitude, and people sensed these things about her. Too many times she caused me to lose customers by butting in just as I was about to close a sale. She couldn't resist showing how desperate she was by saying something like, That looks nice on you. And of course the lady would take one look at Gita's insincere face, take off the dress, and leave the shop. This happened time and again.

Still, I took all I could for about two months, then I told her I was leaving. I told her, I'll tell Desani myself.

And I called him from the corner drugstore and he said, You come on back to my shop, Inez. But I said, No. He'd lied to me. Instead, I went home. And although Desani called me at home, I still wouldn't go back. I was hurt and angry. I felt betrayed by him and angry with Gita.

I stopped by Mama Bradford's. I sat with her at the kitchen table, drinking coffee and telling her how I felt. And she told me to just keep focusing on the positive and to forget the failures. A copy of the *Christian Science Monitor* was folded and lying on the corner of the table. She said, Think about what you've accomplished, Inez, since the children arrived. You have a lot to be proud of, and you'll soon get a good job, too. I knew what Mama Bradford was doing. She was playing the role of a healer.

Feeling better, I went home. At home I didn't tell you about my job problems because you didn't need the pressure, and I didn't even tell Becky that I no longer worked for Desani. She might've worried that I couldn't pay the rent. But I went back to keeping a close eye on the classifieds.

When I called Lowella, she was quick to say I told you so. Bringing those children to Chicago was a mistake, Nez. You should've left them with Mama like I told you. But I shrugged off what she was saying and remembered what Mama Bradford told me: Be positive. And I kept positive. Mind over matter.

Soon I found an acceptable job again as a salesclerk for the Lake Shore Company, working the magazine and cigar counter at the North Shore Railroad Station at Adams and Wabash. Once again, I was employed as a white woman. In applying for the job I didn't say that I wasn't white, but I knew that the job was not open to colored.

I wasn't happy or unhappy about being white. With two children to feed and clothe, I needed to act quickly, and I needed the best paying job I could find, and this was it. I also disliked having Darcy park a block away when he came to pick me up from work. But I well knew the world in which I worked. And by now I well knew the lessons Artie taught me.

Meanwhile, my boss, Mr. Rowe, during my interview, told me that he attended Alcoholics Anonymous meetings, and so did his girlfriend, Sharon, who also worked the counter on a different shift at the station. Mr. Rowe wanted to know if I'd be willing to work the three-to-eleven shift so that they both could go to AA meetings together. I was, and I said yes. Every other week I'd have Saturday and Sunday off, rotating them with Wednesday and Thursday off.

My first time on the job, Mr. Rowe stayed the whole time, to see how I handled the long lines during rush hours when the trains were stopping one right after another. At eleven when we were about to close, he said he was pleased with my work because I was quick and efficient, and that was what counted most.

It was a Saturday night when Darcy stopped by. We were in the living room. He wanted me to lend him money to buy a used car from somebody he was trying to sell a new car. He knew I had money with which to buy my children winter clothes. But where money was concerned, I no longer trusted Darcy since the Jackie Tucker deal. Plus this was hardly the kind of riffraff scene I wanted my children witnessing.

When I told Darcy I didn't have any money for him, he ran into my bedroom. You children stayed in the living room. I quickly followed Darcy. He'd found my purse on the chair at the foot of the bed, and he was emptying it onto my bed. But there was no money there. I was shocked. Seeing him doing that made me fit to tie down. Pointing toward the door, I stood my ground and told him to get out of my house. Now! Right now! I shouted.

He started yelling at me. I thought he had a lot of nerve being mad at me for not giving him my hard-earned savings. So I stood in front of him and kept pointing at the door. Get out, Darcy, or I will kill you, I said. I don't play, I will kill you. I meant it, too. But he refused to move. He kept running off at the mouth about how unfair I was being.

Suddenly I whirled around and headed for the closet just behind me. But before I reached it, I heard him leaving. He went by me like a streak of lightning. By the time I got to the apartment door, Darcy was at the bottom of the stairway. And he and Becky were looking up at me.

I kept my hand behind me and stepped out into the hallway and, looking down at him, and in no uncertain terms, I told him that if he ever came through my doorway again that I would kill him. When I was younger I had been my husband's victim too often. Because of that earlier experience, I was quick—perhaps too quick, some would say—to draw the line. But that was the way I felt. No man was ever going to abuse me like that again.

Darcy called later that night and I said, Darcy, it's over. He called the next day and I told him again that it was over. He kept calling and I kept telling him to forget it, that he was wasting his time. It was definitely over. He said, Girl, I didn't know you go crazy like that. Again, I said, It's over and don't call this number ever again.

When a week went by without a call from Darcy, I thought he'd finally gotten it through his head that it was over, but he called that Saturday morning and said he'd like to stop by to give the children show fare. He said he missed seeing the kids and giving them money for the movies. I started to say, They don't miss you, but I didn't.

I thought about his request, then said, Okay, you can come and park in front of the house, and you can hand them the money from your car window. He said he'd be there in twenty minutes, and when he got there, I went down with you and Serena and stood guard while he handed you the money. I told Darcy, Now that's the last time you're giving my children money for anything. Is that clear? He said he understood. I had my hand in my pocket. He hadn't missed that fact, either. Two or three more calls and he finally gave up.

One night I came home and another tenant—Mavis, who lived in a kitchenette down the hall from us—told me she and her husband had to move. Mavis and I had become friends. Building inspectors, she said, were here earlier today, looking the whole house over for code violations. You said that the inspectors had looked around in our place, too.

Becky was beside herself with anger. She believed her runaway husband had sicced the authorities on her. Chuck was out in Los Angeles, where he was living permanently, and they were having a very disagreeable divorce. He wanted part ownership of the house and some of the profit she was making off it.

I knew we'd have to move soon, but in the meantime, on one of my days off, during the hottest part of that summer, I packed a lunch and took you children to the Brookfield Zoo out in Brookfield, Illinois, to spend the day relaxing and watching the animals. We had fun and in the days that followed the trip to the zoo, I noticed that you and Serena were talking only about the famous gorilla named Bushman. I kept hearing the name Bushman coming up in your conversations. Then I finally caught on. You weren't talking about Bushman at all. It was a code name you'd given Darcy. I tried not to laugh in front of you, but I couldn't help it.

➤

I went to a theater on Fifty-fifth Street to see the then much-talked about movie *Pinky*, starring Jeanne Crain, Ethel Waters and Ethel Barrymore. I cried a lot during that movie. Never before had I been so affected by a movie. It was as though I was watching my own life on the screen. Jeanne Crain, a white actress, was playing the part of a woman who in appearance was white but defined by law as black.

I thought to myself, Funny thing how a white woman, my children's great-grandmother, Rebecca Lankford, can give birth to a black child, but a black woman can never give birth to a white child. I thought about that a long time. The Pinky story was set in the Deep South in the kind of setting I myself had grown up in. And in the days that followed, when I thought about the young woman called Pinky, uncontrollable tears ran down my cheeks. Later, I picked up a paperback copy of the novel *Pinky* and read that, too, and cried some more.

Seventeen

Again my life was about to change in big ways. I could feel it despite the fact that circumstances seemed almost normal. At the same time, another thing resulting from the building inspection was that Mrs. Stonebank had to move.

She'd made arrangements to move in with her granddaughter, Deanna, who, with her husband, lived in the basement apartment, facing the garden on the side. Deanna's baby was only a month old, and Mrs. Stonebank would be able to help.

But this meant that my rent would be eight dollars more. When Becky told me this, I took a deep breath and held it. The room would need furniture, too. Yet the news could have been worse. I felt a sense of relief that I didn't have to go searching for another place. I would find a way to deal with the additional expense. I had no problem with the added space.

In the end, I was able to buy furniture for the new room. It was November and my mind had already turned toward the holidays. You and Serena were now sleeping in twin beds in the new bedroom, and I kept the little bedroom we three had shared. I also bought a floor-model radio and record player for the living room. Up till then we'd had only a tiny radio on a table between the beds in the old bedroom, and the portable TV.

Serena loved the new radio. She used to sit by it and sing along with Doris Day and the Andrews Sisters, and countless other singers. She had a good voice and I liked hearing her sing. Lately she'd been singing "Rudolph, the Red-Nosed Reindeer" a lot, imitating the various singers who sang that song, including Gene Autry. But they were also still playing songs that were around since the end of the war, like "Don't Sit Under the Apple Tree with Anyone Else but Me," and Serena picked those up, too, and belted them out when ever she felt like it.

By now we were getting along all right without Mrs. Stonebank, but I missed her, missed her more than I thought I would. She'd been a lot of company to the children and me, and we'd shared Christmas with her. So I went often down and around to the side door to take her things, part of Sunday's dinner or some fruit. That was a habit of mine when she lived in our back room.

At the same time, I was still a member of one of Mama Bradford's clubs. This one had the long-winded name The Supreme Royal Circle of Friends of the World, and had an office at 104 East Fifty-first Street.

Mama Bradford was chairman and I had been appointed public relations manager.

A big fundraiser dance and social was coming up in mid-January. Mama Bradford wanted me to go downtown with her to help her shop for a new evening gown, and I did. It was sort of like the old days when I lived with her. But I myself was now different. I felt different. Having children with me, I now had new concerns, new interests. I'd become far less material and more spiritual in my thinking. I was growing. I was more practical, less impulsive. Although I'd long been good at it, I was learning how to order my time even better. It all amounted to greater self-discipline and sharper focus on essentials.

The dance was a big affair and a big success. People strutted around and pranced and everybody was polite and regal. At one point I looked at Mama Bradford and thought, How happy she looks! This was Mama Bradford at her best.

One day—years later, in 1957—Mama Bradford called and said, I can't wake Pops up. She sounded out of her mind with fear. I said, I'll be right there. I then told her to go and try again. I got dressed and went upstairs and rang my neighbor's doorbell. I asked her to call the police and give them Sophie Bradford's address. Another one of my neighbors drove a taxi. I was lucky to find him at home, and he rushed me over to Mama Bradford's.

I got there just as the police arrived. I went upstairs

with them. Hugging her, I tried to comfort Mama Bradford. I was trying my best to keep calm. I looked at Pops
lying on his parlor bed covered with the blanket up to
his neck. He looked dead all right, but we had to be
sure.

Odd thing about the sight of him like that: I didn't
feel sadness or fear. He looked so peaceful I couldn't
associate his condition—if he was dead—with misfortune. Although I was not as close to Pops as I was to
Mama Bradford, I felt a warmth toward him that in no
way was less strong than it had been all along. Maybe
it was that even as young as I still was, I was gaining a
greater acceptance of death as a natural part of life.

The police got Pops on a stretcher, and I rode with
them to Providence Hospital. A doctor examined him
carefully and told us he was dead. My heart sank. That
made it official. I felt sad and sick at the same time.

I was always the kind of person who kept my head in
a crisis. Only after the crisis passed did I tend to fall
apart. I wanted to cry, but I needed to stay in control of
myself. I knew Mama Bradford would be in no condition to handle any of the things that now needed to be
done.

I called Leak Funeral Home and arranged for them
to pick up Pops's body. I then went back to try to comfort Mama Bradford as much as I could. I asked her
about Pops's insurance.

She said, Look in the box. When I looked in the box
where they kept their important papers, I couldn't find
any policy for Pops. I said, Mama, where is Pops's life

insurance papers? She didn't know. So I called Pops's agent at Metropolitan Life.

And the agent said, Jeremy Lee Bradford cashed in his policy two years ago. I then asked Mama Bradford for Pops's bank book. She said, Look in the box. And it was in the box. But when I opened the book, I saw that the account had been closed two years before.

All I could do was shake my head in disbelief. I sat down at the kitchen table, with a cup of coffee and a cigarette, to try to figure out the next move. Mama came in and said, Jeremy wanted to be cremated, so why don't you just burn him up, like he said. She kind of laughed.

But I couldn't laugh. I said, Mama, it takes money to cremate a body. She said, Then just throw him out in the backyard. But this time I couldn't help it. I started and couldn't stop laughing. I was hysterical. And now Mama Bradford was laughing, too. Then we were both crying and laughing at the same time.

Finally, I got ahold of myself. I had to arrange for the funeral. I got on the phone and called Pops's relatives in Ohio to tell them he had passed. The only one who could come was his nephew. When the nephew got to Chicago, he rented a car at the airport, then picked me up.

We drove to Mama Bradford's. The nephew said, What kind of funeral do you want for him, Aunt Sophie? She said, He'll be cremated, so don't spend much. The nephew gave her a funny look. Later, he and I drove over to Leak and picked out everything. And the director added up the bill. Contrary to what Mama

Bradford thought, cremation was expensive. The nephew looked at the total and refused to sign the contract. Instead of signing, he said, Send it to Aunt Sophie, she'll sign.

When the nephew and I got back to Mama Bradford's, the house was full of people offering her sympathy. At one point, I went to the bathroom and Mama Bradford came in right after me and closed the door. She whispered, Did he pay? I said, not one red penny. And she just gave me a look.

So I knew I had to act fast or Pops would end up buried by the city in a pauper's unmarked grave. My first stop was at the Palmer House, where Pops had worked as a waiter for many years. I talked with the union man. He appointed one waiter on each shift to take up a collection, and the union man himself brought the money to Mama Bradford.

Then I stopped by the bookie joint where Pops wasted so much of his money trying to get rich quick playing the horses. The bookie man said he would help, and he brought Mama Bradford two hundred dollars that night. Then Pops's sister wired Mama Bradford some money.

When the day of the funeral came I was so exhausted that after I attended the ceremony, I didn't stay at Mama Bradford's for the catered supper, paid for by one of her social clubs. All of her fancy society lady friends were there in their evening gowns, dining by candlelight. Their men were in black or blue suits. It was too much. I couldn't be bothered with it. These people were not in grief. They were having a good time.

Somehow word soon got around that Mama Bradford hadn't had enough money to bury Pops. And this led to friends and would-be friends knocking on her door and asking if she wanted to sell any of her things. She had a flat full of fine antique furniture and art objects. She owned two mink coats, lots of diamonds and gold jewelry. And everybody knew it. When she called me complaining about these people, I told her, Just tell them you are not dead yet.

Yet it seemed that Mama's mind died along with Pops's body. Her grief and disorientation were understandable at first, but after a reasonable amount of time she should have gained some control. All during the day she'd call me about the silliest things. She couldn't get the top off a jar. The phone rang but when she answered nobody said anything. She couldn't manage her money. She didn't know how to write out a check. Pops had always paid all the bills. She seemed totally helpless.

I tried to help, but things got worse. We sat down together at the kitchen table and I mapped out a budget for her. I took my own checkbook out and carefully showed her how to write out a check to pay her bills. But she didn't seem to be paying attention. Instead, she gazed at the wall behind my head. She soon received a notice that her electricity was going to be cut off because she hadn't paid. With the gas company, the same thing. The phone bill was two months overdue. And her life insurance had lapsed since Pops's death.

Nine years later Mama Bradford herself died. Her

death was hard on me, but it was not unexpected. She'd been ill a long time, in a nursing home, and was completely out of her mind. Her sister and her brother's widow came from New York to bury her. Since I had been close to Mama Bradford, I helped them put her affairs in order. But for a long time we couldn't find her life insurance policy. When we found it, her relatives were surprised that she'd left the cash value of it to a woman she hardly knew, a member of one of her clubs.

One of Mama Bradford's club members introduced me to a pleasant and quietly dignified man she called Hayden Wong. I could see that Mr. Wong was certainly a Negro all right, yet he had Asian eyes and a Chinese name. I'd never before met a colored person with a Chinese name, although I'd seen many colored people with Asian eyes.

I had seen Mr. Wong at previous functions over and over since 1945, but before now we had not actually met formally. He was always well dressed and obviously owned his own formal wear—tails, top hat, walking cane, the works. His clothes fit him well. I'd heard that he was a member of Antioch Baptist Church. Obviously popular, he was invited to all the important social gatherings in, and maybe beyond, Mama Bradford's circles.

A few days later, Mama Bradford called me and said that the woman who'd introduced Mr. Wong and me to each other wanted to know if she could give him my telephone number. He wanted it. I told Mama

Bradford to tell the woman to forget it. And that was that. I was not ready or in the mood to start dating. The very idea annoyed me. The problem was not Mr. Wong himself. *I* was the problem, and I knew it.

My boss, Mr. Rowe at Lake Shore, lost his contract with the railway company, and that meant I was out of a job. Those of us who worked at that station were called together, and a man from the main office handed each of us our final check, along with a letter to the unemployment office.

I'd never drawn unemployment. And when I went and found out that the weekly check would be only twenty dollars, I knew that that would not be enough to pay my bills. I needed another job—and quickly.

A day or two later, while in the Royal Circle office, the office manager asked me to consider working full-time for the club as a fundraiser. A big event was scheduled: National Negro Achievement Day.

The club needed as much help as it could find to get ready for the occasion. The projected dates were June twenty-fourth, twenty-fifth and twenty-sixth at the Coliseum on Wabash Avenue. The pay arrangement was acceptable and I would get a percentage of the total dollar amount I raised. With nothing better in sight, I agreed. I could do this and still keep my eyes open for a long-term job.

Using the telephone in the office, I called hundreds of people, attempting to sell booth spaces for the three days. I called a lot of downtown business managers

261

and owners, and got a lot of good responses. I had three months to try to sell all of that Coliseum space. Already I'd agreed to also serve as a host at the exposition. I worked hard and didn't miss any of the many business meetings in the office.

One of the businesses that had purchased space was Hong Kong Cleaners, a chain owned by Argus Ackerman, a white man, who made 90 percent of his money off Negroes. The office manager there, Sol Lodovic, wanted to know about my work plans after the exposition in June. I told him I'd be taking a vacation, then I'd come to work for Hong Kong. He laughed and said that was exactly what he had in mind.

The exposition was a big success. On the second day, Mr. Wong showed up. I was pleased to see him, and as a host, I escorted him around from booth to booth. Before he left, Mr. Wong said, Oh, by the way, would you be interested in going with me to a musical this coming Sunday at my church? The thought appealed to me and I said, Sure, I'd be happy to.

Once the exposition was over, I went to work—as a Negro woman this time—for Hong Kong Cleaners, which had its main office and plant on Forty-third and Wells Avenue. My title? Assistant Production Manager. I was excited about the new job. That a black woman could be hired in such a position was a good sign that working conditions were improving for women and for black people in general. The civil rights movement was just beginning around this time.

Something different was in the air. All the black people I knew felt it.

Hong Kong Cleaners' main plant was a long, low, wide building with two floors, a basement and a parking lot. The main store was on the ground level and it faced Wells. The cleaning went on in the basement. On the second floor were rows of pressing machines, and rows and rows of racks. This was where finished garments hung till the drivers picked them up and loaded them into the fleet of trucks. They were then delivered to the company's dozen or so shops throughout the city.

At Hong Kong, I had several areas of responsibility. I was put in charge of the sewing department, which was on the second floor at one end of the building, where the alterations and repairs were done. Another one of my responsibilities was to oversee the fifteen to twenty pressers doing piecework at any given time. They worked fast at the machines all day. Given my work experience, I knew I was well qualified to do what I was doing.

Taking this job marked the end of my years of working as a white person. That was all behind me now. It was a choice I made, a role I gave up easily now that for the first time as a Negro woman, I was being paid a decent salary. Yet, aside from the fact that I was more than qualified to manage production, I couldn't help but wonder if my light skin had played a role in my being sought out and hired. Getting this job reminded me that among black people, I was never treated in a regular way. I was either punished for having light skin, or I was privileged. Among those white people who saw me as colored, I was treated better than colored folks with darker skin. In any case, I was happy to say good-bye to having to be white just to get a good job. My dream was for a world in which character, as Martin Luther King said, would be the most important thing about a person, not skin color or gender. I was waiting for that world. So far we had only a hint that we might be moving in the right direction.

Eighteen

In the years to come, my life will change dramatically a number of times. I will marry again, have another child—Cassandra—and go into the dry cleaning business with my second husband, Mr. Wong. My marriage and the business both will fail. Years later, I will open another dry cleaning business, Windy City, on the South Side, this one on my own, and it, too, will end during the Chicago riots, following the assassination of Martin Luther King Jr.

And still later, after you and Serena are married and settled into careers—Serena in business and you writing and teaching—I will buy my first house, in the Lake Shore area. Buying the house, for me, will signal a victory over years of money worries. My house will become a haven for my grandchildren—not unlike Mama's house had been for years, for us and for her grandchildren.

A Word of Gratitude

Thanks to Carole Hall for her inspiration and wise advice; thanks to John Talbot and Gail Fortune for their friendship, loyalty, and belief in me and this book; thanks to John Simko for so efficiently seeing the book through production, and to Pam LaBarbiera, the copyeditor, for her careful scrutiny of each word in each sentence; thanks to my sisters and other relatives for their memories; thanks to Pamela for her sensible criticism and devotion; thanks to paid researchers in Georgia; but mainly, thanks to my mother, Inez, for the thousands of conversations she and I have had over the years, for her candor, and her abiding love.

C.M.

About the Author

Clarence Major is a prize-winning poet, novelist and essayist. He is the author of nine novels, including *Dirty Bird Blues; My Amputations* (Western States Book Award, 1986); *Such Was the Season* (a Literary Guild Selection, 1987); and *Painted Turtle: Woman with Guitar* (*New York Times* "Notable Book of the Year" citation, 1988). Author of ten books of poetry, Major was a 1999 finalist for the National Book Award for *Configurations: New and Selected Poems*. Major is also the winner of a 1970 National Council on the Arts Award for his first collection, *Swallow the Lake*. A year later Major's poetry was honored with a New York Cultural Foundation prize. He is a contributor to more than a hundred periodicals, including the *New York Times*, the *Washington Post*, the *Los Angeles Times*, *Essence*, the *Kenyon Review*, *Massachusetts Review*, *Michigan Quarterly Review*, and *The American Poetry Review*, and his poetry and fiction appear in many anthologies, including several *Norton's*. He has served as a literary judge for the National Endowment for the Arts, National Book Awards, and many state and cultural arts agencies. He has read his poetry at the Guggenheim Museum, the Folger Theater, and in hundreds of universities, theaters, and cultural centers in the United States and Europe. In Yugoslavia he represented the United States in 1975 at the International Poetry Festival. He is also editor of anthologies widely used in university classes. Clarence Major lives near Sacramento, California.